THE MAKING OF
THE MODERN
CHRISTMAS

THE MAKING OF
THE MODERN
CHRISTMAS

J.M. Golby and A.W. Purdue

The University of Georgia Press   Athens

To Jessica

who enjoys Christmas

© J. M. Golby and A. W. Purdue 1986.

Published in the United States of America in 1986 by
the University of Georgia Press
Athens, Georgia 30602

First published in Great Britain in 1986 by
B. T. Batsford Ltd

Printed and bound in Great Britain

Library of Congress Cataloging in Publication Data
Golby, J. M. (John M.)
    The making of the modern Christmas.

    Bibliography: p.
    Includes index.
    1. Christmas—United States—History. 2. Christmas—
Great Britain—History. I. Purdue, A. W. (A. William)
II. Title.
GT4986.A1G65 1986   394.2'68282'0941   86-7083
ISBN 0-8203-0879-x

CONTENTS

ACKNOWLEDGEMENTS

In our search for illustrations for this book we have been given enormous help and assistance from a large number of people. In particular we would like to thank Dr Tony Aldgate, Margaret Baber, Tony Coulson, Derek Dalton, Tudor Davies, Mags Golby, Dr Christine King, Anne McGregor, Arthur Meadows and Marie Purdue. Our thanks go also to Sue Cannings, Sue Dowson and Dinah Hill for typing the drafts of the book so quickly and efficiently. Above all, we are deeply indebted to Dr Milo Shott who did so much of the photographic work for the book and who has given us much useful advice.

In addition the authors and publishers would like to thank the following for permission to reproduce illustrations: *Asia Magazine* 1.14; BBC Enterprises 4.28; Chelsea Football Club 4.32; Estate of Norman Rockwell 4.18; Harris Museum, Preston 4.3, 5.16; Harrods 4.4, 4.13, 5.27; IPC Magazines Ltd 1.13, 4.19; Imperial War Museum 2.9, 5.12, 5.14, 5.15, 5.21, 5.22, 5.23; London Transport Museum 4.12; Mary Evans Picture Library 3.15, 4.8, 5.7, colour plate VII; Metropolitan Museum of Art 4.38; National Film Archives London 4.21–4.26, 5.26; Pictorial Press 5.20; The Curtis Publishing Company 4.17; *This England* magazine 1.6; Bettmann Archive/BBC Hulton Picture Library 5.24; Victoria & Albert Museum 2.7, 2.8, 3.35, 3.36, 4.33; The Bridgeman Art Library, colour plates II, III.

COLOUR PLATES

ONE

The Modern 'Traditional' Christmas

Most people, if you were to ask how they preferred to celebrate Christmas, would probably say something like: 'Oh, in the *traditional* way – you know, with turkey and plum pudding and, of course, a Christmas tree; and the children unwrapping the presents from Santa Claus; and carols on the radio or television; Christmas cards from our friends all round the room; and with the house full of relations, because my parents always come, and my husband's mother and his brother Bob . . . Well it's really a time for the family isn't it, and especially for children?'

Whenever Christmas is discussed, invariably at some point the word 'traditional' is used. It is a word which reveals just how deeply entrenched the festival is as an annual institution, and the idea of a traditional Christmas produces an immediately understood picture of the way in which we spend, or would like to spend, our Christmas Day. It conjures up a vision of family gatherings, warm homes, presents, Christmas trees, decorations and a special Christmas dinner. Of course, the programme of events on Christmas Day varies from family to family. Some people open their presents first thing on Christmas morning, others wait until after Christmas dinner. Some families eat their Christmas dinner at lunchtime, others sit down to the meal in the late afternoon, and so on. Very often these particular local family traditions, which exist within the larger overall Christmas tradition, thrive because members of the family have attempted consciously to preserve the past of their childhood. The reason for this, quite simply, is that Christmas is above all a time when children become the focus of attention, and childhood memories are enduring.

So, the strongest emphases of this 'traditional' Christmas are undoubtedly on the home, the family and particularly the children, but the elements of good-fellowship and charity are also present, and for some it is still primarily a time to remember and celebrate the birth of Christ. In addition, there is also built into the festival a strong element of nostalgia: a feeling that somehow past Christmases were happier, more enjoyable and, well, 'more like Christmas'. Perhaps this is not surprising. After all, if Christmas is a time when children are given special attention, then it is understandable that childhood memories of Christmas will be particularly vivid and exciting and that there will be determined attempts to recreate happy past Christmases. Such idealised retrospection is sharpened by dislocated circumstances and it is no accident that very often Christmas assumes a heightened importance at times of trouble, whether this be within the family or on a national scale. The absence of a loved

one at Christmas is mourned by a family gathering, while for those who are away from home through no fault of their own – as in the trenches in 1915, in the Ardennes in 1945 or in Vietnam in 1972 – Christmas Day is the one above all others when men and women yearn to be back in their own country and with their own families.

Bound up with celebration is a strong desire to recapture the atmosphere of Christmases of the past. But were the old Christmases really better? 'Nowadays we depend too much on the telly'; 'We used to make our own amusements'; 'Christmas is too commercialised'. These or many other similar statements have been made, not just in recent years, but in every decade of the century. On Christmas Day 1912 a leader in *The Times* regretted that,

> We have lost the art of commanding our feelings so as to fit them to the season; and still more the art of making our pleasures without the help of professional entertainers. . . . Now we have separated very sharply the secular from the sacred part of Christmas.

1.2 Christmas is a time particularly for the children: 'Watching for Santa Claus'. *Illustrated London News*, Christmas Supplement 1893

Der father crismus
we are sending
a list of things wot
we wood lic
for crismus

for the man sed
if we did not
rit soon we wood
not get wot we
wontid for crismus

1.3 Child's letter to Father Christmas

1.4 Christmas is not a time for the lonely: 'The young man who is alone on Christmas Day'. *Illustrated London News*, 21 December 1850

1.5 Christmas is a time when the poor and unfortunate are remembered: 'Christmas in a workhouse'. Note the deferential sentiments on the back wall. *Graphic*, 25 December 1876

The writer looked back with envy to 'the Dickens Christmas with its high spirits and simple pleasures', and, certainly, in tracing the history of Christmas it is around the time of Charles Dickens in Britain and Washington Irving in the United States that Christmas takes on the particular characteristics that we associate with it today. Alongside the age-old traditions of charity, the Victorians installed the belief that Christmas is a time for the celebration of families and for the indulgence of children, and, perhaps most interestingly of all, they also built into the festival a nostalgia for Christmas past. For, whereas today we look back to the age of Washington Irving and Charles Dickens as a time when Christmas really *was* Christmas, so both these writers and their contemporaries were searching for an ideal Christmas somewhere in *their* past. Dickens in his *Sketches by Boz* points out that some 'people will tell you that Christmas is not to them what it used to be'. The author of the *History of the Christmas Festival*, published in 1843, also wrote of earlier days 'when good old customs were thought more of than at present, and Christmas kept up with greater hospitality'. Even earlier in the century Sir Walter Scott's poem *Marmion* recalled a time when

England was merry England, when
Old Christmas brought his sports again,
'Twas Christmas broached the mightiest ale;
'Twas Christmas told the merriest tale;
A Christmas gambol oft could cheer
The poor man's heart through half the year.

It is impossible, however, to find any period when this ideal Christmas actually existed. What both Dickens and Irving were helping to create was an idealised version of Merrie England rather than any real medieval Christmas. Nevertheless, despite their hankerings for past Christmases, the Christmas that we know and observe today is very much the creation of the Victorians in Britain and the United States. Not only did they fashion it but they gave it a centrality in the yearly cycle which it had never known before.

Christmas is now irrevocably our major annual festival. It is an institution: a date eagerly anticipated by hundreds of millions. A National Opinion Poll survey in 1975 revealed that 88% of adults expected to have a happy Christmas; and, if other surveys are anything to go by, it is clear that a large percentage both in Britain and the United States celebrate the festival by spending Christmas Day in a 'traditional' manner, that is, with their immediate family.

But the Christmas rituals that we enact are comparatively modern, just over

1.6 Present-day nostalgia: advertisement for *This England* magazine, Winter 1981. The advertisement reads, 'Recapture the spirit of England this Christmas . . . These modern times can easily mar your memory of what Christmas used to be like in the England of yesteryear – a family affair with simple joys and inexpensive gifts . . .'

1.7 'Christmas of the Past 1580'. *Illustrated London News*, 31 December 1859. Victorians yearned to capture the spirit of past Christmases

1.8 . . . but they saw a continuity of Christmas sentiment into their own time: 'Christmas of the present, 1859'. *Illustrated London News*, 31 December 1859

one hundred years old. Of course, since the nineteenth century the festival of Christmas has grown enormously in scale: although this may not be reflected in observance of it as a religious festival, it most certainly is in the numbers who participate in the secular celebrations and the extent to which industry, commerce and the media are geared towards catering for the Christmas festival. Nevertheless, despite the growth of Christmas, its essential characteristics remain very similar to those established in the nineteenth century – namely, its emphasis on family, children, goodwill and nostalgia.

Because these Victorian Christmas values are nowadays continually reinforced by industry and the media, some argue that it has become virtually impossible to ignore Christmas or to celebrate it in any other than the most predictable ways. While to some the very predictability of the festival is one of its virtues, for others it can loom as a burdensome ritual. A few years ago a tongue-in-cheek article in the *Daily Mirror* on Christmas Eve suggested '20 ways to stop going crackers' on Christmas Day. Directed at housewives, on whom the burden of Christmas Day so often falls, it advocated amongst other things that the reader should,

> Resist the temptation to say 'bloody Christmas'. Instead start cooking . . .
> Ignore totally any whines or whinges from the kids as they compare the quality or quantity of presents . . .
> Say silently: 'This is the season of goodwill to all men, including his mother' . . .

CHRISTMAS CARDS,

AT

CHAPMAN'S,

54, LEICESTER-SQUARE, W.C.

CATALOGUES POST-FREE.

No. 3330.—FLOWERS and VIEWS.

Charming compositions of landscapes and flowers, suggestive of the seasons. Verses on back by Frances Ridley Havergal. Size, 5½ by 4. The set of four, 9d.

No. 3393.—FLOWERS FREE and SAFE by POST.

Three designs of violets, primroses, and snowdrops, as if inclosed in an envelope. An unique novelty. Size, 3½ by 4¼. The set of three, 7d.

No. 3366.—ROUGH RUSTICS.

Bold and bright studies in oil of village children, with wishes, such as "Long may you live, and me to see you." Size, 7 by 4. The set of three, 7d.

No. 3107.—HUMOROUS GATHERINGS FROM THE ANIMAL WORLD,

Illustrating the words "A Christmas Greeting to you." Three clever sketches—"The Puppy and the Chicken," "The Kitten and the Crab," and "A Very Strange Bird." Size, 3½ by 5. The set of three, 2½d.

No. 3307a.—CLEVER KITTENS.

Two remarkably droll designs of kittens climbing a ladder and climbing a tree; folding into convenient form, with decorative covers. Size, closed, 4¼ by 3. The set of two, 4½d.

No. 3492.—BETHLEHEM.

Reproductions from ivory paintings of the Shepherds, the Magi, the Presentation in the Temple, and the Holy Family at Home, with Scripture references. Size, 5½ by 5. The set of four, 1s.

No. 639.—FAIRY GLIMPSES.

Highly attractive and pleasing delineations of fairy gambols in sea and air, from original water-colour drawings, by Miss E. G. THOMSON. Size, 6½ by 4¼. The set of three, 1s. 3d.

1.9 By the second half of the nineteenth century newspapers and magazines were printing large numbers of Christmas advertisements, from classified ads like this one in the *Illustrated London News* of 17 November 1883 for Christmas cards . . .

1.10 ... to large display adverts. *Illustrated London News*, Christmas Supplement 1893

1.11 Remedies for over-indulgence: Eno's fruit salts advertisement

1.12 A famous Pears' Soap advertisement, Christmas 1897

Pampered, Pretty, Practical, Preposterous... Presents for Pets

Never before has there been such an amazing range of goodies for our furred and feathered friends—designer dog clothes, a rustic kennel, bed baskets and a beautifully shaped bird cage, plus Christmas stockings full of toys and treats. By Sue Brown

All the details of where to buy are over the page

1.13 Nowadays it is not just people who are on the receiving end of Christmas presents. Advertisement in *Woman*, 22 December 1984

When umpteenth member of family has asked what is wrong with your face and why you are so miserable, pick up telephone, ring British Airways and confirm single booking on flight BA 257 from Heathrow to Antigua, Barbados and Port of Spain . . .

The final recommendation may reflect the secret fantasies of many in the lead-up to Christmas, but in the last resort, even the most irascible and short-tempered usually make some sort of effort to observe the festival. Evelyn Waugh, spending Christmas 1946 at home with his wife and four children, recorded in his diary: 'I made a fair show of geniality throughout the day though the spectacle of a litter of shoddy toys and half eaten sweets sickened me . . . A ghastly day'.

Despite complaints about standardisation and commercialisation, it would be foolish to ignore the fact that millions of individuals, not only in Britain and the United States, but in many other parts of the world, make a conscious decision to observe the rituals of Christmas in general and of their own family in particular. The continuation of Christmas is just as much a result of our own desires and actions as of compelling commercial forces.

Christmas, our major festival, is celebrated by devout Christians, by those of luke-warm faith and by non-believers. The reasons for its abiding appeal go far beyond a desire for a massive annual celebration. They are to be found, amid paradox and in the presence of many Christmas Pasts, in the central dilemmas of mortal man. It is the central argument of this book that the festival was extensively reworked and reinterpreted during the nineteenth century to meet the needs of modern urban society; yet, like every vital tradition, it is built upon foundations which, like rock formations, contain layers from different ages. The old Christmas, which Victorians so admired, even while they changed it so radically, was itself the result of Christianity's partial incorporation of and partial coexistence with the old pagan Winter Feast. We, as we turn the central heating up another notch and watch the children unwrap their complex modern toys, are also recognising the frailty and resilience of humanity, the mysteries of trees, seasons and fire and, whether we believe in it literally or not, the hope contained in the Christian Nativity.

1.14 Christmas shopping is something that is now done the world over. *Asia Magazine*, 20 November 1983

TWO

The Old Christmas

There has always, in Europe, been a great winter festival. There were good material reasons for having a last great feast at which, before the onset of the most severe weather, all but carefully conserved stocks of salted meat and cereals were consumed. Yet, as G.K. Chesterton recognised, such feasting and merrymaking when the worst hardships were to come were essentially acts of defiance:

> It is the element not merely of contrast, but actually of antagonism. . . . Man chooses when he wishes to be most joyful the very moment when the whole material universe is most sad. It is this contradiction and mystical defiance which gives a quality of manliness and reality to the old winter feasts which is not characteristic of the sunny felicities of the Earthly Paradise.

But the winter festivals of pre-Christian Europe were not puny and insensate gestures against the season and the unconscious powers of wind and snow. They were rather an affirmation of man's relationship with the forces of nature and his ability to placate and encourage them; the celebrations had a religious purpose.

The old winter festivals dramatised the death of the Old Year and the beginning of the New. At a time when the sun appeared in decline and when winter threatened the survival of the community, the celebrations were attempts to propitiate the mysterious forces responsible for the coming of the bleak season and to encourage the return of life-giving sun and fertility. They were, indeed, fertility rites as well as feasts and the food consumed was at once a meal and a sacrifice. It is in this context that we can understand the importance of lights and fires to these festivals, for they were seen as assisting the revival of the sun, while evergreens were no mere decorative embellishments but symbols of the continuity of life, at a time when other trees and plants appeared dead.

We can distinguish between two main streams of pagan customs, those of southern Europe and those associated with the Yule of the Teutonic North. The most important mid-winter festivals of the later Roman Empire were Saturnalia, which began on 17 December, the Kalends, which began on 1st January and the Birthday of the Unconquered Sun, which was on 25 December. Saturnalia was named after an early Roman god, Saturnus, whose name means 'plenty' or 'bounty' and the festival was accompanied by general revelry, feasting and drunkenness. During Saturnalia and the Kalends which inaugurated the new year, buildings were brightly lit and decorated with evergreens, processions crowded the streets and presents were exchanged. The feasting was presided

2.1 'Merry Christmas': this illustration captures the delight in eating and drinking which was embedded in mid-winter revelry from the earliest of times. *Illustrated London News*, 20 December 1845

over by a mock ruler or Master of the Revels, and normal customs and social roles were reversed: masters waited on their servants, pastimes like gambling – which were forbidden at other times – were permitted, men dressed in animal skins or put on women's clothes, while women dressed as men. There was a place in the Roman festive season for children too and Juvenilia was the special feast of children.

In the midst of these weeks of revelry came a day set aside for the celebration of the sun whose annual crisis at the Winter Solstice was so much the cause of these winter festivals. Although generally celebrated, the Day of the Birth of the Unconquered Sun was in particular the great feast-day of the Mithraic religion, one of the greatest of the 'mystery religions' of the Roman Empire, secret and exclusive but highly influential because so many of its adherents were army officers and businessmen. Mithraism was a great rival to Christianity in the late Roman Empire and it was perhaps in tacit recognition of its influence that, when the Christian church eventually decided to celebrate the birth of Christ, it should have chosen 25 December as the date.

The northern European festival of Yuletide had many similarities to these southern festivities. There was the same gargantuan feasting and the wassailing and carousing of the Germanic tribes was as copious and boisterous as the drinking and revelry of the Romans; the emphasis upon the lighting of great fires was at the same time a ritual encouragement to the waning sun and an inseparable part of festive cheer in the cold northern forests. There was a peculiar north-European preoccupation with the dark forces of the night during

2.2 The Victorian idea of a pagan Christmas: 'Christmas in the Saxon times'. *Illustrated London News*, 24 December 1859

Yuletide; not only were northern mid-winter nights long and sometimes frightening outside the Yuletide but the special season was supposed to liberate ghosts and demons from their normal restrictions. Odin himself became a Yule-demon; in Scandinavia 'Julebuk' appeared in a devilish mask and horns yet, strangely, also brought gifts to children; while in parts of Germany a similar hideous monster has lived on to modern times as Klausauf, a companion to St Nicholas in his seasonal visitations to children. It is from Yuletide that many of the associations of our Christmas come: the warmth and good cheer around the Yule log, while outside there is darkness, cold and 'things that go bump in the night'.

Early Christians did not celebrate the birth of Christ. Birthdays in themselves were associated with pagan practices; the Gospels say nothing about the actual date of Christ's birth, and within the early church the second coming of Christ was expected imminently, so the incarnation may well have seemed of lesser importance. It was not until the fourth century that Christmas was officially established as a feast of the church by Julius I, Bishop of Rome, although it had almost certainly been celebrated before then. Christmas is, in fact, the classic example of the Christian church coming to terms with the traditional customs and rites of the people, superimposing a Christian festival upon the pagan mid-winter holiday. However, we find from the beginning an ambiguity in the attitude of fervent Christians to the festive season; there is an emphasis upon the fact that it is Christian and, with Easter, the most important of the festivals, yet, at the same time, there is an uneasy feeling that many aspects of the celebration

2.3 The flower of chivalry celebrate: the Victorian conception of Christmas at the Court of King Arthur. *Illustrated London News*, 23 December 1865

are worldly or pagan.

Thus we find St Gregory Nazianzen, who died in AD 389, warning his flock against '. . . feasting to excess, dancing and crowning the doors' and urging 'the celebration of the festival after an heavenly and not after an earthly manner'. Many a priest, prelate or minister has preached to his congregation in similar vein, from AD 389 to AD 1986. The 'gross' elements of Christmas – gluttony, drunkenness and the challenge to public order and discipline represented by indecent plays, the reversal of social roles and dressing up as the opposite sex or as animals – all became the standard targets of austere and reformist prelates. The fear that the 'true spirit of Christmas' and the central miracle of the Christian religion – God becoming man – were in danger of being lost amidst the revelry of Saturnalia, or Yuletide, has been perceived since Christianity first chose to celebrate the birth of its Saviour at that time and season.

In Anglo-Saxon England the Christian festival dovetailed easily into existing pagan practices, for 25 December was the beginning of the Anglo-Saxon year and the time of the Yule festivities. Pope Gregory the Great was an enthusiastic advocate of the policy of assisting proselytisation and conversion by coming to terms with old customs and rites, recognising that people were not easily weaned from their old traditions. As he wrote to St Augustine when the latter had embarked on his mission to England, the old festivities of the 'killing time' could be used by Christianity:

> Nor let them now sacrifice animals to the Devil, but to the praise of God kill animals for their own eating, and render thanks to the Giver of all things for their abundance; so that while some outward joys are retained for them, they may the more easily respond to inward joys. For from obdurate minds it is undoubtedly impossible to cut off everything at once, because he who strives to ascend to the highest places rises by degrees or steps and not by leaps.

Yet despite Pope Gregory's hopes, the pagan elements in the Anglo-Saxon mid-winter feast probably remained for the majority stronger than the Christian embellishments. Viking invasions reinvigorated pagan traditions, while priests were scarce and often as illiterate as their flocks. Away from the influence of prelates and monasteries, it is likely that the Yuletide tradition remained strong and that the mid-winter feast remained substantially what it had been before the coming of Christianity, a time of heavy drinking and carousing among blazing Yule logs in buildings adorned with evergreens. Many of the customs accompanying the festivities – the mummers' plays whose usual theme was a dramatic presentation of death and resurrection, the wassailing of fruit trees by pouring ale upon them, and even the pastimes which have become our blind man's buff and leap frog – were, consciously or unconsciously, derived from fertility rites.

In Britain, the festival was to remain, despite the Church's best efforts, obstinately pagan. To some extent Christmas (and the term seems first to have been used in Britain on the eve of the Norman Conquest) can be seen as ground contested between the high culture of an elite and the popular culture of the common people. Ecclesiastical opinion would view the sensual enjoyment of Christmas festivities and of the many pagan customs, either as the necessary indulgence of the weak and fallible, or as dangerous distractions from Christian worship. Yet the secular élite joined enthusiastically in the popular Christmas,

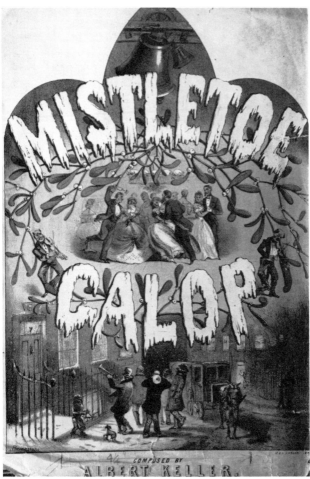

2.4 The use of evergreens for
the decoration of houses
continues today. Christmas
wreath on the front door of a
house in Rockland County,
New York State

2.5 The old pagan emphasis
on evergreens was taken up
by the Victorians. Mistletoe
was used extensively in house
decorations and, in this
instance, as a theme for a
Christmas dance

2.6 The old custom of
bringing in the boar's head.
In Scandinavian legend, the
wild boar was a favoured
animal, sacrificed to Freya,
goddess of love and fertility

and the greater wealth of Norman kings and nobles, and their distance from subjects and vassals, were expressed in Christmas festivities not different in content from those of the populace, but distinguished by their grandeur and conspicuous expenditure.

The feast which King John gave at Christmas 1213 is supposed to have surpassed the most sumptuous and gargantuan banquetry of previous years, but the celebrations of Henry III were on an even grander scale. In 1252 he entertained a thousand knights and peers at York; so expensive was the feast that the Archbishop of York alone gave 600 fat oxen and £2,700 towards the feasting. A century and a half later, Richard II provided 2,000 oxen and 200 tuns of wine for the 10,000 who dined daily at his expense. It was incumbent upon barons and lesser magnates to dispense hospitality and provide cheer to the extent that their resources would allow. Such boundless hospitality was more than simply generosity to friends and supporters and philanthropy to inferiors, for Christmas celebrations fulfilled a political and social purpose. They enhanced the reputation of hosts, could bind together alliances and strengthen feudal bonds; they were probably essential to the survival of poorer retainers and peasants during the bleakest time of the year. Present giving, which was an established part of such festivities, also underwrote feudal relationships: to give to a feudal superior implied fidelity, while the giving from superior to inferior was something of an obligation.

Another important aspect of Christmas festivities was that they provided a release from the normal social rules and allowed authority to be symbolically overturned. The old Saturnalian customs of cross-dressing in the clothes of the opposite sex or putting on the skins of animals continued to be associated with Christmas, as did the prevalence of gambling at this time and the practice of superiors waiting upon those of inferior rank, which survives to this day in the British army. The elections of boy bishops and Lords of Misrule are customs which appear to have become popular in the fourteenth century. They are a formalisation of the essential topsy-turveydom of Christmas; in schools, colleges and churches boy bishops were installed, while at the courts of kings and nobles, Lords of Misrule or Christmas Lords were appointed. Lords of Misrule were usually persons of humble rank and were often jesters or fools of court or manor. For the season the world was turned upside down – a necessary release from the disciplines of rank and place which prevailed at other times but one which could yet, by violent paradox, draw attention to the importance of that same rank and discipline. Such respites from the norm are not always easily contained or controlled, however psychologically necessary they may be, and it is not surprising that they often resulted in serious disorder, a fact that was to give the Puritans of the sixteenth and seventeenth centuries a useful ancillary argument in their attack upon Christmas.

The medieval church made a serious attempt both to ensure that the more pagan and popular aspects of Christmas were contained and harnessed within the Christmas festival, and to popularise specifically Christian aspects of Christmas. Old Christmas customs could be reinterpreted by the Church, in the way that holly came to be seen as a symbolic reminder of Christ's crown of thorns, for example, but more important was the retelling of the story of the Nativity in terms accessible to the common people. That the English Christmas remained for long less Christian than the Christmases of continental countries, is

2.7 The old custom of cross-dressing is an obstinate
survivor in British culture.
Here George Robey is
dressed as a pantomime
dame

26

27

suggested by the fact that there is no evidence for the cult of the crib in the old English Christmas, and that the Nativity play and the carol were both foreign importations. Nativity plays began in churches, as seasonal embellishments to the liturgy, and then passed from churches to the streets and from the clergy to the laity, losing the Latin language and becoming popular and vernacular in the process. The carol made an opposite journey: from its origin in popular French dance songs, condemned by the church as lustful and pagan and associated with Christmas only by the season in which it was sung, to a genre which was primarily religious, with many examples being written by the clergy for use in church, as with this fourteenth-century example:

2.8 Clarice Mayne dressed as Dick Whittington

2.9 Another ancient custom which survives today: Christmas dinner in the army. The Officer Commanding, Major J. Irvine, serves the youngest soldier, Private Ash, first. 25 December 1944 (Imperial War Museum)

Iesu, swete sone dere!
　On porful bed list thou here,
And that me greveth sore;
For thi cradel is ase a bere, [byre]
Oxe and asse beth thi fere; [companion]
　Weepe ich mai tharfore.

Poor, rural people were profoundly affected by the concept of a prince born in poverty, surrounded by beasts which miraculously fell on their knees before him, and attended by shepherds.

Despite the best and most creative endeavours of the Church, the essentially secular nature of the English Christmas persisted and was to endure into Tudor and Stuart times. The Twelve Days of Christmas were the main national holiday and were observed as a time for feasting, dancing, singing, sporting, gambling and general excess and indulgence. Religion as well as custom could be held to give authority for the seasonal extravagance, but the ethos, almost the morality, of Christmas was that people should be merry and hospitable; if they were also inclined to be prayerful, then well and good.

As we have seen, there had been from the beginning divided counsels among churchmen as to the attitude to take towards Christmas; whether to accept that mortal and fallible men needed their annual period of excess and licence and that all was well provided this took place under the mantle of an ostensibly Christian purpose, or whether to disapprove of and to attempt to eradicate all that was not essentially Christian in the festivities. But a sterner Puritan tradition was to arise with the Reformation which condemned, not merely secular excess, but Christmas itself. Previous reformers had sought to rid the festivals of their pagan manifestations and origins but, with the Reformation and the divisions in the western Christian tradition, many now sought to

2.10 'Christmas Masque at the Court of Charles II'. *Illustrated London News*, 24 December 1859

eradicate all Popish practices, which included all feast days. That sturdy man of the people, Martin Luther, had a fondness for Christmas, but the Calvinist tradition condemned it; there was no authority to be found for its observance in the Bible. In Scotland John Knox condemned Christmas along with all the other festivals of the Church; and during the Tudor period in England there were attacks on the main national holiday from Puritans, though these were motivated by a mixture of outrage at its licence and excess and disapproval of the festival itself.

The Tudor and Stuart age in England is notable for being both the high period of the Old Christmas and the setting for a chorus of dissent which reached its climax with the attempt to abolish the festival during the Commonwealth. Christmas had never before been so lavishly and flamboyantly celebrated as at the courts of Tudor and Stuart monarchs, with masques, mummeries, theatres and pageants. Henry VIII delighted in the extravagance and the buffoonery of Christmas celebrations; Queen Mary saw the 'traditional' Christmas as invested with the full authority of Roman Catholicism; Queen Elizabeth 'gambled' with loaded dice and in 1597 'the head of the Church of England was to be seen in her old age dancing three or four gaillards' at Christmas. James I was not over-fond of the Calvinism that had gripped his native land and in his time the court of St James was full of seasonal merriment and ablaze with masques, revels, gambling and fantastic entertainment.

Beyond the court and the festivities to be found in great houses, lesser manors and humble farmhouses, there were the murmurings and dissent of Puritanism. Christmas became the focus of a debate about the nature of religion and the proper purpose of society. Claims were made that Christmas time had become a

season of un-Christian practices: 'there is nothing else used but cards, dice, tables, masking, mumming, bowling, and such like folleries'; such practices, it was suggested, were derived via Popery from Saturnalia, and Christmas could more truly 'be stiled Divels-Masse, or Saturnes-Masse (for such *too many make it*) than Christmasse; there being farre more affinitie betweene the Divell, Saturne, Masse, and the riotous Christmas-keeping, than betweene Christ and them . . .'.

To some contemporaries Old Christmas seemed to have other enemies than Puritan religiosity. The sixteenth and early seventeenth centuries saw economic distress and a drift from the countryside, exacerbated by several years of poor harvests; at the same time the paternalist sense of duty in the upper ranks of society, which could be seen as a prerequisite for social order, appeared to be weakening. In much contemporary writing Old Christmas became a symbol for hospitality towards the poor, an understanding between the different levels of society, and happier and more prosperous times in now neglected villages. A ballad of the late sixteenth century, *Christmas's Lamentation for the losse of his acquaintance; showing how he is first to leave the country and come to London*, regrets that the nobility now feast in London at Christmas, neglecting their country houses and the rural poor:

> Houses where music was wont to ring,
> Nothing but bats and owlets do sing.
>   [and]
> Places where Christmas Revels did keep
> Are now become habitations for sheep.

Both Queen Elizabeth and James I ordered the nobility and gentry to return to

2.11 The tradition of the Baronial Hall maintained in Stuart times

2.12 Old style Christmas
charity: charity dispensed
from the big house was
central to the old rural
Christmas

2.13 The vindication of
Christmas: an anonymous
seventeenth-century
broadsheet

their estates and keep hospitality among their neighbours.

The attempt by the Commonwealth to abolish Christmas is one of those curious episodes in human history in which governments attempt to change national mores and almost human nature itself by legislation. Some have compared it to Prohibition in twentieth-century America. The attack upon Christmas came at a time when the testimony of poets and other writers makes it clear how important Christmas was to the mass of the population. Robert Herrick, whose writing was based upon his experience as a country vicar, eulogised the merriment and hospitality of the festival:

> Come, bring with a noise,
> My merrie merrie boyes,
> The Christmas hog to the firing;
> While my good Dame, she
> Bids ye all be free;
> And drink to your hearts desiring.

The English Puritans certainly disapproved of much that went on at Christmas but only a minority wished to abolish the festival itself. It was pressure from their Scottish Presbyterian allies that brought about the ordinance of 1644, proclaiming that Christmas Day should be kept as a fast and a penance rather than as a feast. For a dozen years the traditional Christmas festivities were prohibited: Parliament sat on Christmas Day, its soldiers attempted to ensure that shops were open, and the churches remained closed while evergreen decorations were prohibited.

There was widespread opposition to and defiance of the interdiction of Christmas and despite the efforts of the authorities, vigorous in some areas but half-hearted in others, the festival continued to be celebrated. As a Puritan MP told the House of Commons, 'The people of England do hate to be reformed . . . . These poor simple creatures are mad after superstitious festivals, after unholy holidays'. The Commonwealth gave a considerable boost to Royalist propaganda in trying to ban Christmas. It was a blessing to Royalist pamphleteers, who could associate the Old Christmas and old Father Christmas with their cause, and the resolution passed by ten thousand men of Kent and Canterbury that, 'if they could not have their Christmas Day, they would have the King back on his throne', suggests that the cause of Christmas may have played a far from negligible part in the Restoration of the crown.

These quarrels and disputes were central to the early American Christmas, for the colonists took with them not only many of the traditions of their native lands but the dissensions of the homelands as well. The religious and secular features of the traditional Christmas were early planted on American soil, but the different religious persuasions of the settlers resulted in America mirroring Britain and Europe in the varied attitudes taken towards the festival.

In Virginia, Christmas was observed in style as early as 1607, when Captain John Smith and his men kept it 'among the savages' with 'plenty of good Oysters, Fish, Flesh, *Wilde Fowl* and good bread'. The Episcopalian and Cavalier loyalties of many of the settlers ensured that, as the colony grew and prospered, its Christmas festivities resembled those of the Old English Christmas – save, perhaps, that the fecundity of their rich land enabled them to surpass English Christmases in the lavish nature of their entertainment and the variety

of food under which their banqueting tables groaned.

From the middle of December until Twelfth Night, Virginian country gentlemen feasted and dispensed generous hospitality. They burned Yule logs, sang carols, decorated their churches and houses with garlands of evergreens and rang the church bells, while it soon became a southern custom to hail the season by shooting fire-arms and letting off fire-crackers. Their days were filled with shooting and fox-hunting or with indoor amusements such as billiards and cards, while at balls and parties in the evenings there was dancing and yet more card playing. Their dining, usually in the late afternoon, was both formal and sumptuous. In addition to the traditional fare of saddles of mutton, rounds of beef, hams, geese and plum-puddings, the New World provided turkeys, Indian corn, potatoes and sweet potatoes. Virginian Christmases were indeed a worthy transplantation of Old Christmas and Merrie England!

Things were very different in New England, for Puritans there shared the hostile attitude of their English co-religionists to Christmas, seeing its religious celebration as 'Popish' and the secular festivities as a 'wanton Bacchanalian Feast'. The Pilgrims spent their first Christmas Day working on the erection of a building and partook of their customary plain meal. Following the example of the Commonwealth, which had, as we have seen, declared 25 December a day of fast and penance in 1644, and then forbidden the observance of Christmas, Easter and Whitsuntide (none of these having been specifically ordained by the Bible), the American Puritans enacted a law in the General Court of Massachusetts to punish those who kept Christmas:

> ...anybody who is found observing, by abstinence from labor, feasting, or any other way, any such days as Christmas day, shall pay for every such offence five shillings.

Even after the law was repealed in 1681 the festival was largely ignored in much of New England: the shops remained open, people went about their normal business and there were no special church services. Governor Edmund Andros had to be escorted by two soldiers when he attended a church service – held in Boston Town Hall because no church was available – in 1686, while a Christmas service in the Anglican King's Chapel in 1706 was disrupted by a shouting mob who broke the windows. New England was not to enter enthusiastically into Christmas celebrations until late in the nineteenth century. As the New England bred Henry Ward Beecher put it in 1874, 'To me, Christmas is a foreign day...'

If the Puritan attack upon the English Christmas encountered sturdy opposition from the populace, and if the Restoration of 1660 ensured that the laws against Christmas were abolished, there can, nevertheless, be little doubt that the seventeenth century marked a significant diminution in the importance of the festival. Old Christmas never quite came back in his former health. From the Restoration until the nineteenth century there was a waning of Christmas, interrupted by self-conscious attempts to maintain its traditions. After the Commonwealth, Christmas ceased to be celebrated in the same grand style, at such length and with such munificent hospitality at the Court or in the great homes. To much of the population, especially in country districts, Christmas still appeared a pleasure, a duty and a right; and to more old fashioned country squires, especially those of Tory outlook, the maintenance of its traditions was a worthwhile religious, social and political gesture; but it made far less appeal to the well-to-do in urban areas or to the broad middle ranks of society. The

2.14 'The Cavalier's Toast': in this Victorian reconstruction the cavalier may well be toasting the serving maids and the spirit of Christmas. *Illustrated London News*, Christmas Supplement 1897

CHRISTMASS DAY.

Mark here the Merchants Family,
With their own Chaplain disagree:
His Pride exceeds his hunger far
No Grace he'll say because they jar:

The Butler with mischeivous Look
A Christmas Gambol gives the Cock:
Down on the Floor she tumbles flat
With melted Butter scalds the Cat.

The Groom behind the Kitchen Door,
By force makes harmless Nell a Whore:
The Baker's Boy his Pleasure spies
Lets fall the Voider with the Pies:

The Monkey too must have a Pull,
To interrupt the wanton Call.
The Black views all with cunning Grin.
Now look this Medley oer again.

Published according to Act of Parliament by P. Griffin Fleet Street December 26 price 6.d

2.15 These eighteenth-century cartoons suggest both that Christmas revelry and mischief continued into that century and that cartoonists found it a ready source of satire

Church of England distanced itself from many Christmas traditions along with so much else of popular culture and practice.

Many factors contributed to the slow decline of the Christmas festival from its only partially successful revival in the late seventeenth century: an antipathetic theology, changes in agricultural practice, the enlarged importance of manufacturing and commerce, and a distaste among sections of educated society for the antic and irrational aspects of Christmas. By the early nineteenth century the traditions of the festival were crumbling and passing into desuetude – a development reflected in the increasing nostalgia which pervaded accounts of Christmas festivities and gave impetus to the foraging out and collecting, by folklorists and antiquarians, of Christmas legends and archaic practices.

The maps of settlement of European religious sects largely determined American attitudes to Christmas until the nineteenth century. In general Puritans, Baptists, Presbyterians and Quakers strongly opposed the observance of Christmas while members of the Church of England, the Dutch Reformed Church, Lutherans and Roman Catholics celebrated the festival. New York inherited from New Amsterdam an enthusiastic appreciation of the festive season, and season it was, for Christmas Day itself was merely the climax of weeks of merrymaking which for the Dutch burghers began on St Nicholas's Eve, 5 December, when the saint on his white horse arrived with presents and sweetmeats for children. In New York it was a time of which Puritans might well disapprove; the daughters of Governor Trumball of Connecticut, for instance,

CHRISTMAS GAMBOLS; OR A KISS UNDER THE MISTLETOE

wrote home in 1800 of the 'sweet Christmas kisses' they had received.

2.16 Cartoon published 1784

In much of eighteenth-century America, apart from the contrasts between Virginian merrymaking at one extreme and the anti-Christmas feeling in the centres of New England Puritanism at the other, there was a divide between town and country when it came to the celebration of Christmas. Whereas in England the countryside might appear to be the heartland of Christmas, in America it was often the towns, where wealthy merchants and professionals were frequently Anglicans: so it was that in Philadelphia Christmas was much celebrated in the eighteenth century, despite the large numbers of Quakers living both in the city and outside it. Both Lutherans and members of the Dutch Reformed Church, however, kept up the festival in parts of the Pennsylvanian countryside.

The American Revolution and War of Independence may well have slowed down the development of a more united attitude towards Christmas, for there was a tendency to identify its celebration with the Church of England and therefore with Toryism and Loyalism. Religious, social and, perhaps, class differences found expression in disagreement over Christmas. Increased immigration from Germany brought further support for it but the large number of immigrants from Calvinist Scotland and Northern Ireland probably redressed the balance. The separation of Church and State established by the American constitution in 1791 may nevertheless have taken much of the political animosity out of attitudes towards Christmas, for its celebration could no longer be said to symbolise the dominance of the Church of England. Indeed, from the late eighteenth century onwards we can discern Christmas as having become less a theological battleground, and more of a secular or folk festival which most churches sought to harness or incorporate.

Christmas in late eighteenth-century America was increasingly popular, yet it remained fragmented and inchoate, the heir of a host of national and religious traditions as well as of the age-old desire for a revivifying celebration at mid-winter. It was to find a new unity and purpose in the nineteenth century, when the secular and folk elements in the festival were rewoven and reinterpreted to suit the needs of a modern, increasingly urban society. As religious passions cooled, all but the most narrow and unworldly of these sects and churches, who had opposed the celebration of Christ's birth, were impelled to follow their congregations in reluctantly recognising Christmas. The many national traditions which together formed an emergent American consciousness and culture played their part in the development of the new American Christmas, but the cross-fertilisation between America and England was to be the crucial factor in shaping the Anglo-American Christmas which in its essentials was to become the modern international Christmas. No-one is more associated with the development of the American Christmas tradition than Washington Irving, yet it was to the Old Christmas of England that he turned for inspiration; on the other side of the Atlantic, no-one is more associated with the modern English Christmas than Charles Dickens, but it was in America that he found many of his most appreciative audiences. Our Christmas draws selectively upon a host of European traditions but was nevertheless forged by Anglo-American cultural exchange in the early and mid-nineteenth century.

2.17 'Christmas Greens': Thomas Nast entwines, in this mid-nineteenth-century illustration, the specifically Christian symbol of the cross, the old customs connected with the revivifying properties of evergreens and the modern preoccupation with the charm and innocence of children

2.18 Randolph Caldecott's illustration of Washington Irving's romanticised old English Christmas. 'Never did Christmas board display a more goodly and gracious assemblage of countenances.'

THREE

The Victorians and the Refurbishing of Christmas

Christmas, in the first decades of the nineteenth century, was neither a major event in the calendar nor a popular festival. Few magazines or newspapers referred to the festal day in any detail and many ignored it completely. In 1790 the leader writer in *The Times* had asserted that, 'within the last half century this annual time of festivity has lost much of its original mirth and hospitality' and that newspaper's attention to the festival over the next half century bears witness to its general decline; in twenty of the years between 1790 and 1835 *The Times* did not mention Christmas at all, and for the remaining years its reports were extremely brief and uninformative.

Robert Southey thought that the festival had become merely a matter of eating seasonal food and that, were it not for the children's interest in plum cakes and puddings, even this would soon be discontinued:

> All persons say how differently this season was observed in their fathers' day, and speak of old ceremonies and old festivities as things which are obsolete. The cause is obvious. In large towns the population is continually shifting; a new settler neither continues the customs of his own province in a place where they would be strange, nor adopts those which he finds, because they are strange to him, and thus all local differences are wearing out. In the country, estates are purchased by new men, by the manufacturing and mercantile aristocracy who have no family customs to keep up,

3.1 The old: Norfolk coach at Christmas

3.2 The new: 'Arrival of the Christmas train. Eastern County Railway'. *Illustrated London News*, 21 December 1850

3.3 A selection of Randolph Caldecott's illustrations for Washington Irving's *Old Christmas*: hospitality for the locals at Bracebridge Hall

3.4 Christmas Eve at
Bracebridge Hall (Caldecott)

3.4 Christmas Eve at
Bracebridge Hall (Caldecott)

3.5 Christmas Dinner
(Caldecott)

and by planters from the West Indies, and adventurers from the East who have no
feeling connected with times and seasons which they have so long ceased to observe.
(*Letters from England, 1807*)

Yet, from the mid 1830s onwards, we can detect a resurgence of interest on the
part of the newspapers and periodicals who had previously ignored Christmas,
and the festival quickly became an annual topic for discussion and illustration.
Southey was correct in seeing urbanisation and a more mobile population as
erosive of old customs and as tending to iron out regional differences. What he
and many others failed to foresee was that the very consciousness of change and
of the fading of old traditions would combine with the needs and preoccupations
of the new, more industrial and urban society, to produce a new Christmas as
central to the lives of the population as its predecessors.

It was laments for the waning of the old Christmas and retrospective
celebrations of its merriment and good cheer which proved to be harbingers of
the festival's new vitality. Washington Irving provided an imaginative
reconstruction of a Christmas he saw as resembling 'those picturesque morsels of
Gothic architecture which we see crumbling in various parts of the country,
partly dilapidated by the waste of ages, and partly lost in the additions and

alterations of later days'. The 'Old Christmas' at Bracebridge Hall was set in the present of the early nineteenth century, but was a conscious attempt to recapture the customs and traditions of earlier centuries, which even the alert antiquarianism of Squire Bracebridge could make no better than a facsimile. Charles Dickens's description of Christmas at Dingley Dell in *Pickwick Papers* is an idealisation of an eighteenth-century Christmas, a 'good humoured Christmas'. Together, the 'Old Christmas' of Irving's *Sketch Book* (1818) and *Pickwick Papers* (1836) provide an enduring imagery of Christmas which is annually reiterated in Christmas cards and festive illustrations, where jovial squires entertain friends and retainers by roaring fires, and stout coachmen, swathed in greatcoats, urge horses down snow-covered lanes as they bring anticipatory guests and homesick relations to their welcoming destinations.

Despite this nostalgia, the eighteenth century, in which early nineteenth-century writers so often located a hey-day of Christmas, had not been, as we saw in the previous chapter, a period in which Christmas was particularly popular.

In the 1760s, when the Bank of England was closed for 47 days during the year, it was just one of many holidays. For many people it was not an exceptional occasion and for some it was not as important a festival as New Year or even St Valentine's Day. The development of the Victorian Christmas, which was initiated by a nostalgia for a half-imaginary recent past, was not a revival, for the Christmas which Victorians sought to recapture drew selectively upon many Christmases past; it was a symbiosis of an idealised past with the preoccupations of Victorians themselves and was so extensively refurbished and reinterpreted that it amounts to an invented tradition.

The sections of early nineteenth-century British society which responded most enthusiastically to the nostalgia for the old traditions of Christmas were not themselves central to the Christmas whose passing they regretted. It was the middle ranks of society, themselves rarely depicted in the Christmas scenes of country house celebrations and coaching inns which so enraptured them, and who had during the seventeenth and eighteenth centuries often been associated with opposition to the festival or many of its manifestations, who became its most ardent champions. The aristocracy and gentry did in the early years of the century celebrate Christmas, at least to the extent of going to church on Christmas day and enjoying a special dinner, while many held country house parties over the festive period and maintained the customs of giving presents of clothing, blankets or coal to their tenants. But, as the *Gentleman's Magazine* of 1824 pointed out, it was not so much the upper classes as the 'middle ranks' of society who were the real upholders of the Christmas festivities. We cannot be sure exactly who the magazine writer would have included in his 'middling ranks': whatever the definition, the range of incomes, inequalities of status and varieties of ways of life encompassed by such a broad categorisation are bound to have been enormous. What the established professions of medicine, the law and the church had in common with bankers, merchants or factory owners, or what any of them shared with clerks or small shopkeepers, was much less than their location in a very broad social spectrum between manual labour and landed wealth would suggest. Yet, contemporaries were insistent on the expansion and growing importance of what some were beginning to call the 'middle classes' and, with all their heterogeneity, the life styles, moral and political attitudes and burgeoning consumer demands of these groups were crucial in shaping the institutions and values of an increasingly urban society. Charles Dickens would have included himself among the 'middle ranks' and it was to this varied readership that he, like most popular writers of his day, directed his work.

Dickens returned time and again to the theme of Christmas. It is tempting to see him as almost the inventor of the Victorian Christmas, but there were others also writing about the Christmas season. A short story by Harriet Martineau was published in 1834, in which her heroine talks of Christmas in the country which 'had always been a season of merriment to her, and to all the household. She always had some cousins to stay with her then . . . and nothing but pleasure was thought of for the whole week . . .' Dickens's role was more that of the skilful populariser who embedded the themes and associations of Christmas in settings accessible to his readership.

Dickens brought together the mutually supportive preoccupations of nostalgia for a colourful but stable past, where easier and more convivial social relationships were exemplified by Christmas festivities, and anxiety about a rapidly changing present with its many moral and social problems. The evocation of Christmas in *Pickwick Papers* is hardly original; the nostalgia for merry old Christmas had already been given its definitive literary form by Washington Irving, who was in turn greatly influenced by Sir Walter Scott's historical romanticism. *A Christmas Carol* (1843) is, however, one of the greatest Christmas texts for in it Christmas becomes a bridge between the world as it is and the world as it should be, and here we are at the heart not only of the Victorian Christmas but of the modern Christmas as it has continued to develop. Mr Pickwick's Christmas at Dingley Dell was a Christmas Past, but Scrooge's Christmas pointed to the social problems of the present and anxieties about the future.

The charges most frequently made about the Victorians relate to their hypocrisy and sentimentality, but hypocrisy may be seen as a baffled recognition of dilemmas, and sentiment as an exaggerated empathy with others which caricatures them as our best but least fortunate selves. Christmas in Dickens's novels stands as a metaphor for human sympathy and, because its appeal is associated with childhood, family and tenderness, it harnesses

3.8 Perhaps the most well-known of all Christmas story characters: John Leech's illustration of Scrooge and Bob Cratchit

sentiment and imagination with consummate effectiveness. In Dickens's last novel, *The Mystery of Edwin Drood* (1870), Drood is murdered on Christmas Eve and the crime is thus made to appear the more dreadful by the contrast it makes with the normal associations of the day.

Washington Irving and Charles Dickens link the two countries which together evolved the modern Christmas. Irving epitomises that long tradition of American interest in the traditions and antiquities of an older society. His descriptions of the old Christmas were popular in both Britain and the United States. In *The Sketch Book*, Irving depicted the excitement of schoolchildren journeying homeward for the Christmas holiday, a theme that rapidly became standard in Christmas literature. The following description of schoolboys returning to Philadelphia at Christmas time, written for the American Sunday School Union in 1830, is almost an exact echo of Irving:

> The stage passed rapidly along the fine turnpike road; and at dusk the blowing of the horn announced their near approach to the great city; soon the coachman's whip was thrown on top of the stage, a loud ring at the door of their father's dwelling was answered by the servant; the boys beheld the cheerful lighted hall and were soon embraced in the arms of their parents and sisters, who ran out of the parlour to receive them. The parlour too was lighted, not only with lamps, but by a blazing hickory fire, for it was a cold, frosty evening, toward the end of December.

3.9 *A Christmas Carol*: 'Mr Fezziwig's Ball' (John Leech)

3.10 One of the most popular of all Victorian Christmas scenes, the Christmas coach: 'Country road scene in winter'. *Illustrated London News*, 21 December 1850

The philosophy of Christmas expressed by Dickens in *A Christmas Carol* was given an enthusiastic reception in America and the book and numerous dramatisations of it were to become part of the American Christmas. Dickens himself gave a number of readings of *A Christmas Carol* in the United States and made a great impact upon his audiences, even in the areas of New England where a puritan antipathy to Christmas lingered. One result of his reading at Boston on Christmas Eve 1867 was the 'conversion' of a New England manufacturer:

> Among the multitude that surged out of the building came a Mr and Mrs Fairbanks (the former was the head of a large-scale factory), who had journeyed from Johnsburg, Vermont, for the occasion. Returning to their apartments in Boston, Mrs Fairbanks observed that her husband was particularly silent and absorbed in thought, while his face bore an expression of unusual seriousness. She ventured some remark which he did not appear to notice. Later, as he continued to gaze into the fire, she inquired the cause of his reverie, to which he replied: 'I feel that after listening to Mr Dickens's reading of *A Christmas Carol* tonight I should break the custom we have hitherto observed of opening the works on Christmas Day'.
>
> Upon the morrow they were closed. The following year a further custom was established, when not only were the works closed on Christmas Day, but each and every factory had received the gift of a turkey.

The Dickensian Christmas was an illumination of both the contentments and the anxieties of the Victorian middle classes. These were the sections of society who were expanding and growing in prosperity on the crest of economic and social change. Yet the Victorian attitude towards change was ambivalent; from one point of view it was seen as synonymous with progress, but from another as a dislocation of traditional values leaving more questions than answers, more problems than solutions, in its wake. The growing middle class included many who had only just arrived in their new social position and had, inevitably, a sense of their own insecurity in that position; behind pride in newly won status, the walls of the new villa and insistence upon the security and privacy of the family, lay deep doubts as to the durability of it all. Nor could the experience of other sections of the population be ignored or shut out. Whatever the overall benefits of industrialisation and urbanisation, it cannot be denied that in the short term they brought hardships and dislocation for many. What marks early Victorian society is not its disregard of social problems but, in contrast to previous societies, its consciousness of them. It was a consciousness not characterised solely by altruism, for it was also concentrated by fear. From the period of the French Revolution until the late 1840s, there was a groundswell of discontent erupting at times into violent protest. Although in retrospect the chances of a revolution in Britain during these years were slim, the middle and upper classes were at times genuinely alarmed and fearful of attacks on their property.

America in the mid-nineteenth century remained much more of a rural and agricultural society than did Britain, but it was also a society conscious of rapid change as its territory, its population, its economy and its cities all expanded rapidly. Many Americans were uneasy at the challenge to the traditional values of a nation of small farmers and artisans represented by the growth of cities, of business and industry, and by the accelerating influx of immigrants with different values, cultures and religions. The problems of how to preserve social

3.11 The Victorian Christmas 'was an illumination of both the contentments and the anxieties' of the middle classes. Contentment: 'A Christmas party: rich'. *Illustrated London News*, 25 December 1886

cohesion and how to resolve the contrast between the American dream and an often flawed reality were to be further exacerbated by the Civil War.

In both countries the new importance of Christmas and its reinterpretation developed in a context of growing prosperity, where many of the middle classes had more money to spend than ever before, and yet against a back-drop of social unease. It was in such circumstances that the Victorian middle classes started to renovate and refurbish Christmas and to give the festival the essential characteristics that it retains today. In part, they copied the behaviour and customs of the past, and especially those of the English upper class, but they also added new elements to the festival, and reinterpreted it in the light of their own preoccupations. These preoccupations were the opportunities and problems of increased wealth and leisure time, a growing belief in the importance of the

3.12 Anxiety: 'A Christmas party: poor'. *Illustrated London News*, 25 December 1886

3.13 'Children acquired a special place in the Victorian Christmas': 'The Private View'. *Illustrated London News*, 23 December 1865

family unit and, despite the material benefit that industrialisation was bringing to them, a reaction against the ugliness of some of these developments, the obvious poverty of the unemployed and unskilled, and the threat of social conflict.

In these circumstances home and family, and security and privacy to safeguard them, became of prime importance to middle class Victorians. So Christmas became something of a celebration of the family unit. As Dickens himself put it in his *Sketches by Boz*: 'A Christmas family party! We know nothing more delightful!' Yet another occasion for celebrating hearth and home was discovered. True, the Christmas house parties of the aristocracy and gentry had included the family, but the family gathering was not its central purpose and children had not been given the place at Christmas time that was allocated to them by middle class Victorian parents. It is often alleged that the Victorian middle classes invented the concept of childhood (though the doll's houses and toys of earlier periods cast doubt on this); even if they did not, they certainly coloured it with the further ingredient of innocence. Children acquired a special place in the Victorian Christmas.

This use of Christmas to celebrate the family, and indulge its children, can be seen as an example of the tendency within the urban middle classes to make social life and leisure more private. But here we come to that mixture of guilt, fear and genuine philanthropy that made up the Victorian social conscience. If the family was good and children were innocent, you could not celebrate them without considering the hierarchy of families which stretched from the Royals down to the Cratchits. How did Christmas relate to the wider community, and did it have any relevance at all in breaking down class barriers?

The Victorians found the answer through two devices. The first built on the tradition of previous centuries and saw Christmas as a time when the poorer and deserving members of the community should be remembered. The Victorian middle classes put much effort into giving to the poor at Christmas and into pointing out who the needy were. Pictures and stories depicting the poor at this time of year became the staple ingredient in the growing number of Christmas books and magazines which were published from the mid-1830s onwards. An early Christmas edition of *Punch* in 1843 contained Thomas Hood's 'Song of the Shirt', a fierce denunciation of the sweated industries. This social conscience helps to explain the instant success of *A Christmas Carol* (1843), which sold some 15,000 copies in its first year of publication, while nine London theatres staged dramatised versions of the story in 1844 alone.

Perhaps just as prevalent, and as central to the idea of the Victorian Christmas as pictures and stories of the poor, were the tales and legends of merry, jovial, pre-Puritan Christmases where all classes met together in revelry and entertainment. The romantic antiquarianism of the Victorians found in Christmas a perfect subject, and the Victorian middle classes looked back with longing to idealised Christmases past. But the idealisation of the past was more than just this; it also contained a second remedy for the problem of social division. It had the merit of fitting in well with the theme of goodwill, benevolence and charity towards the poor. For the Christmases of the past were depicted as times which were socially harmonious, where all classes met together to celebrate the festival of Christmas. This ideal was captured perfectly by the writer of *Christmas in the Olden Times* published in 1859:

THE SONG OF THE SHIRT.

WITH fingers weary and worn,
  With eyelids heavy and red,
A Woman sat, in unwomanly rags,
  Plying her needle and thread—
    Stitch! stitch! stitch!
In poverty, hunger, and dirt,
  And still with a voice of dolorous pitch
She sang the "Song of the Shirt!"

  "Work! work! work!
While the cock is crowing aloof!
  And work—work—work,
Till the stars shine through the roof!
It 's O! to be a slave
  Along with the barbarous Turk,
Where woman has never a soul to save,
  If this is Christian work!

  "Work—work—work
Till the brain begins to swim;
  Work—work—work
Till the eyes are heavy and dim!
Seam, and gusset, and band,
  Band, and gusset, and seam,
    Till over the buttons I fall asleep,
  And sew them on in a dream!

"O! Men, with Sisters dear!
  O! Men! with Mothers and Wives!
It is not linen you 're wearing out,
  But human creatures' lives!
    Stitch—stitch—stitch,
In poverty, hunger, and dirt,
Sewing at once, with a double thread,
  A Shroud as well as a Shirt.

"But why do I talk of Death?
  That Phantom of grisly bone,
I hardly fear his terrible shape,
  It seems so like my own—
  It seems so like my own,
  Because of the fasts I keep,
Oh! God! that bread should be so dear,
  And flesh and blood so cheap!

"Work—work—work!
  My labour never flags;
And what are its wages? A bed of straw,
  A crust of bread—and rags.

That shatter'd roof—and this naked floor—
  A table—a broken chair—
And a wall so blank, my shadow I thank
  For sometimes falling there!

  "Work—work—work!
From weary chime to chime,
  Work—work—work—
As prisoners work for crime!
  Band, and gusset, and seam,
  Seam, and gusset, and band,
Till the heart is sick, and the brain benumb'd,
  As well as the weary hand.

  "Work—work—work,
In the dull December light,
  And work—work—work,
When the weather is warm and bright—
While underneath the eaves
  The brooding swallows cling
As if to show me their sunny backs
  And twit me with the spring.

"Oh! but to breathe the breath
Of the cowslip and primrose sweet—
  With the sky above my head,
And the grass beneath my feet,
For only one short hour
  To feel as I used to feel,
Before I knew the woes of want
  And the walk that costs a meal!

"Oh but for one short hour!
  A respite however brief!
No blessed leisure for Love or Hope,
  But only time for Grief!
A little weeping would ease my heart,
  But in their briny bed
My tears must stop, for every drop
  Hinders needle and thread!

With fingers weary and worn,
  With eyelids heavy and red,
A Woman sate in unwomanly rags,
  Plying her needle and thread—
    Stitch! stitch! stitch!
In poverty, hunger, and dirt,
And still with a voice of dolorous pitch,
Would that its tone could reach the Rich!
  She sang this "Song of the Shirt!"

3.14 'A fierce denunciation
of the sweated industries':
Thomas Hood's 'Song of the
Shirt', printed in *Punch*,
December 1843

3.15 The idealisation of
Christmas past: 'Christmas in
the Baronial Hall in Olden
Times'. *Illustrated London
News*, 24 December 1859

Time was when the frost was on the pane, and snow lay thick upon the ground, when
all the chimneys smoked and all the ovens were full ... when all were full of gladness
and both serf and squire, baron and retainer, did their very best to keep their
companions happy. All classes gave themselves up to frolic and revelry, with a
thoroughness of spirit.

The Victorians were beguiled by what G.K. Chesterton was to call 'that
feudal Christmas' but the imagery of the drawings from the *Illustrated London
News* and many other popular magazines, together with the evidence from
Christmas cards and a whole host of other Victorian sources, tells us that what
the Victorians bequeathed to us was not really a revival of a mediaeval or feudal
festival. What they invented was Merrie England or Olde England – the
eighteenth century with an idealised mediaeval ethic. It consists of a world of
benevolent squires, stage coaches, inns and ruddy-faced landlords. It sought to

3.16 Charity for the poor in the country: 'A Cottager's Christmas'. *Graphic*, 25 December 1877

3.17 A Christmas Dinner for Manchester Newsboys, 1874 (Mary Evans Picture Library)

3.18 Even more worrying was the plight of the town slum dwellers: 'Strangers', *Punch*, 29 December 1883

bring an idealised past to the rescue of an uneasy and insecure present, and to melt the problems of a rapidly changing and sometimes ugly society in the warm glow of Christmas cheer and goodwill. The Christmas bells of Tennyson's *In Memoriam* were able to vanquish all manner of evils:

> Ring out the grief that saps the mind,
>   For those that here we see no more;
>   Ring out the feud of rich and poor,
> Ring in redress to all mankind.
>
> Ring out a slowly dying cause,
>   And ancient forms of party strife;
>   Ring in the nobler modes of life,
> With sweeter manners, purer laws.
>
> Ring out the want, the care, the sin,
>   The faithless coldness of the times;
>   Ring out, ring out my mournful rhymes,
> But ring the fuller minstrel in.

3.19 Victorian Christmas charity: a typically sentimental picture loved by Victorians, 'Outdoor Relief'. *Illustrated London News* 23 December 1865

Such a Christmas could never be 'what it used to be' for it had, of course, never been, and it is not surprising if so many Victorian writers complained that Christmas was not so enjoyable nor so whole-heartedly observed as in the past. Yet it was like so much else in Victorian society – the railway station behind a Gothic façade – only superficially an exercise in nostalgia. The invented tradition which was the Victorian Christmas catered for many aspects of that dynamic society: it provided a season for conspicuous and extravagant consumption such as all societies feel to be necessary from time to time but which was now attended to by expanding retail and leisure industries; it provided a focus for the celebration of family, community and nation; and, despite the hypocrisies and moral myopia, it came to be a time for taking stock of social progress, for measuring the actual against the ideal and insisting that harmony and conciliation were, perhaps only for the season, not unattainable. It is one of the myths of modern times that the healthy and progressive society celebrates itself and its moment in its artefacts and institutions and has no need to cloak itself in tradition, real or imaginery. The truly inventive society refurbishes its present with an ideal past. The enduring modern Christmas, developed in its essentials in the first half of the nineteenth century, is a testimony to the Victorian genius.

If the essential contribution of the Victorians to the modern Christmas was their reinterpretation of its meaning and spirit, the customs, myths and newly-minted traditions with which they embellished and symbolised the festival are scarcely less important. A relentless antiquarianism failed to re-establish in the barren soil of the nineteenth century the customs of the old English Christmas: Yule logs were unsuitable for modern fire-places, wassail bowls too hearty for

some Victorian heads and stomachs, Lords of Misrule too impish and unruly for nineteenth-century propriety, while boar's heads were hard to come by and not much appreciated in any case. As one Victorian writer acknowledged, 'Instead of toast and ale, we content ourselves with sherry and chestnuts, and we must put up with coffee and fragrant tea, instead of having the old Wassail-bowl'. The boar's head was replaced by 'the roast beef of old England, a turkey or a goose', together with a plum pudding, all of which ornamented 'the table of the peasant or artisan, for which he had during some previous weeks been preparing'.

The importation of geese and turkeys in large quantities from France and Germany from the 1840s on meant that Leadenhall and Newgate markets in London were packed with poultry in the week before Christmas. Most families made some effort to prepare a special Christmas dinner and to this end many working families subscribed to 'goose clubs'. By contributing 3d or 6d a week from September onwards a member of the club would be entitled to a goose and, perhaps, a bottle of spirits.

Although the menu was different by the Victorian period, the Christmas dinner had always been a traditional part of the festival. This was not the case with the Christmas card, the Christmas tree, the cracker and Santa Claus, all of which were Victorian innovations.

The Christmas carol is a partial exception to this list because many old carols were rescued as they were about to die out. The custom of the singing of carols by 'the waits', originally the bellmen and waits who cried out or announced with music the watches of the night, had been attenuated and debased. Although some waits in the City of Westminster had still an official existence, waits in early nineteenth-century England were largely seasonal mendicants with a repertoire

3.20 'An ambuscade' while collecting evergreens for Christmas. *Illustrated London News*, Christmas Supplement 1893

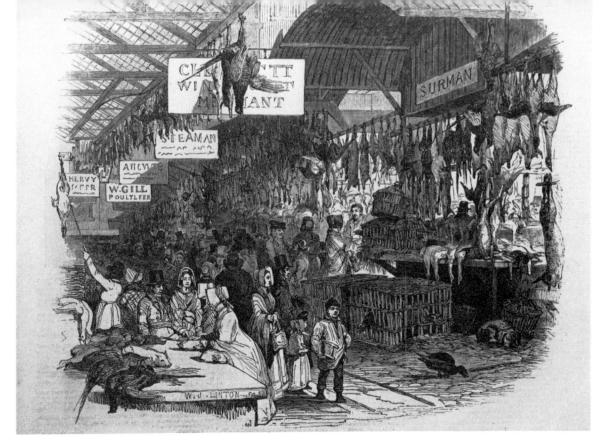

3.21 Leadenhall Market,
London. *Illustrated London
News*, 27 December 1845

3.22 Newgate Market,
London, on Christmas Eve.
Illustrated London News, 27
December 1845

3.23 The goose club was an
important working class
institution: Phiz's illustration
of 'The Goose Club'.
Illustrated London News, 24
December 1850

3.24 'A prize from the
Christmas Goose Club'.
Graphic, 21 December 1872

limited in both number of carols and verses to individual carols. Neither had the Church of England proved a worthy custodian of the carol, for few carols were sung in churches at Christmas time. Carolling and carols may well have been better preserved in rural and small town America. From the 1850s onwards strenuous efforts were made to revive the carol. The research of antiquarians and the systematic collection of folk songs recovered many carols that were in danger of being forgotten. Clergymen attempted to make carol singing a part of Christmas worship and books of carols for church use were published.

Outside the church carol singing became increasingly popular. John O'Niell, a power-loom weaver from Clitheroe, wrote in his diary on Christmas Day 1856 that he was visited by two sets of singers; and George Horrocks, a cotton manufacturer from Farnworth in Lancashire, wrote to his son at Christmas 1861 about '4 sets of singers during Xmas eve' including one group who 'wheeled a harmonium about from house to house'.

In the second half of the century many new carols were written. *Christmas Carols Old and New*, published in 1871, contained 42 carols, the majority of which were by contemporaries. By the end of the century the carol was integral to Christmas; its setting was as often church or home as the open air, for most religious denominations in both Britain and America encouraged its use in church services, while many carols were well suited to the piano in the parlour and to family harmony. Both greed and altruism ensured, however, that the tradition of the waits would continue, either in the shape of itinerant groups of hopeful children taking their few verses from door to door, or of small choirs collecting for churches or charities.

The Christmas tree was established as the centre-piece of Christmas in American and British homes in the middle decades of the nineteenth century. The combination of lights and evergreens brought together two very old aspects of Christmas, but the astonishing speed with which a custom, hitherto important only in some parts of Germany, became an instant tradition, not only in America and Britain but in many European countries, suggests that it symbolised the preoccupation of the new Victorian Christmas. The tree was at the centre of a *family* Christmas and it dominated the *home*; it appealed especially to children and represented the new importance given to the indulgence of children at Christmas time; and it was used to embellish the custom of giving presents within the family and to friends, presents being attached to the tree or laid underneath it.

In both Britain and America the Christmas tree was introduced by German immigrants. Pennsylvanian Germans brought the Christmas tree with them to America and in the 1830s and '40s the custom of decorating trees spread rapidly in the United States. The German background of the British royal family ensured that they were amongst the first to adopt the custom in Britain, and trees were introduced to the courts of George III and William IV. German merchants at Manchester had their Christmas trees in the 1830s. It was, however, the adoption of the practice by Queen Victoria and Prince Albert which gave a massive boost to the Christmas tree and soon established it as an integral part of Christmas. It is fitting that the royal couple who placed such an emphasis upon the virtues of family life should have played an important part in the introduction of what came to symbolise the family Christmas. Victoria and Albert set up their trees for the first time at Windsor in 1840 and in 1848 the *Illustrated London News* printed what is one of the most famous of nineteenth century Christmas scenes, Victoria and her family beside their Christmas tree; the same illustration was used by *Godey's Lady's Book* in America in 1850 though the couple are *incognito* and Victoria's tiara is removed. Dickens was naturally enthusiastic about the 'pretty German toy' and imagined, in a contribution to *Household Words* in 1854, that from its branches there came a message: 'This is in commemoration of the law of love and kindness, mercy and compassion. This is in remembrance of ME'.

So, within a very short space of time, the Victorians had established the tradition of the Christmas tree. In the *Christmas Tree* annual of 1857, a book of 'instruction and amusement for young people', one of the contributors 'recalled' a particular Christmas when he was young:

> At a signal from my mother, we followed her into the dining room on the other side of the passage . . . on the table in the centre there was placed a great Christmas Tree hung all over with little lamps and bon-bons and toys and sweetmeats and bags of cakes. It was the first tree of the kind that I and my companions had ever seen. It was quite a new fashion the Christmas tree; and my brother Tom who had just come home from Germany had superintended its getting up and decoration . . .

3.26 One of the most of
famous of all Christmas
illustrations: 'Christmas tree
at Windsor Castle'. *Illustrated
London News*, 23 December
1848

No wonder then that by the end of the century it seemed that the tree had always
been part of Christmas and that a description of President Harrison's Christmas
at the White House in 1891 refers to 'an old fashioned Christmas tree for the
grandchildren'.

The Christmas tree was not the only form of greenery used to decorate
Christmas festivities: the holly, the ivy and the mistletoe maintained their place.
The kissing branch or bough had been, previous to the Christmas tree, the
centrepiece of Christmas decor in many English homes, with its lighted candles
stuck in apples and its branch of mistletoe. Though such boughs were largely
replaced by the Christmas tree, mistletoe itself enjoyed considerable popularity

in the Victorian period. At the beginning of the century mistletoe and the custom of kissing under it were more often found in cottages or in the servants' quarters, but they quickly ascended the social ladder. A mid-century *Punch* cartoon depicts the ladies at a fashionable party attempting to kiss the few eligible males. Judging by the amount of coy and heavy-handed humour on the subject of mistletoe in *Punch* and other periodicals, the opportunities afforded by the plant loomed large in the Victorian consciousness. Here was a rare opportunity, hallowed by ritual, to avoid the proprieties of the age – to kiss and embrace out of wedlock and often across the barriers set by age, group or class. To an age used to the mini-saturnalia of the office party it may seem a brief and fleeting opportunity, but it was one gladly taken, amid much nudging and merriment.

The popularity of mistletoe gives us one glimpse of the old spirit of the Lord of Misrule peeping from behind the crinoline of the Victorian Christmas; the pantomime, which grew in popularity to become a major part of Christmas

3.28 Thomas Nast's 'Cutting
Mistletoe in the South'

3.29 'Under the Mistletoe'.
Punch, December 1852

3.30 Thomas Nast's
'Christmas Flirtation'

3.31 The jokes about
mistletoe continued. *Punch*, 25
December 1935

3.32 (p. 66) One important
aspect of pantomime was the
elaborate scenery and
intricate technical devices
which made so many scene
changes possible: scenes from
London Christmas
pantomimes, 1859

3.33 (p. 67) Scenes from
London Christmas
pantomimes. *Illustrated London
News*, 24 December 1859

"IF YOU'RE NOT USING THE MISTLETOE, MADAM, MAY WE BORROW IT
DOWNSTAIRS FOR HALF-AN-HOUR?"

DRURY LANE

ADELPHI

LYCEUM

66

COVENT GARDEN

HAYMARKET

ST JAMES'S

67

entertainment in England, gives another. A marvellously anarchic form of popular art, the pantomime moved away from its original format of Pierrot and Columbine to become a fairy story interpolated with sketches and songs from the music hall repertoire of the day. It has remained a peculiarly British form of entertainment, and in the figures of the Dame (played by a male comedian) and the Principal Boy (a leading actress or female variety star) we can discern, by the end of the nineteenth century, the old Christmas practice of impersonating the opposite sex.

The Christmas card was a British invention. Christmas greetings had long been exchanged orally and in letters; with the development of cheap printing the Christmas card evolved as a means of sending Christmas messages to those one might not see and to whom one would not usually write. Its utility, in short, seems obvious: only the most basic of literary skills were needed to send a card and one could maintain the warmest of greetings with the minimum of effort. A precedent of sorts existed in the Valentine card and also in the custom of Christmas pieces – specially printed writing paper upon which schoolchildren exercised their best copper-plate handwriting.

There is some dispute as to who invented the Christmas card but it is usually accepted that the first was one designed by H.C. Horsley, R.A., following a suggestion made by Henry Cole, and published by the latter in 1843. It shows a family Christmas dinner with three generations present, the party toasting the recipient as 'absent friend'; side panels depict the theme of Christmas charity with the poor being fed and given clothing. Other examples from the 1840s are cards by W.C.T. Dobson, the painter, and W.M. Edgley, an engraver, but the

3.34 Leech's illustration of 'Going to the Pantomime'. *Illustrated London News*, 24 December 1853

3.35 Dan Leno as Mother Goose, Drury Lane theatre, December 1902

3.36 Rita Presano as Prince Racket in Jack and the Beanstalk, Drury Lane theatre, December 1899

3.37 The first Christmas card, 1843, designed by H.C. Horsley

WITH FOND WISHES FOR A MERRY CHRISTMAS.

3.38 Late nineteenth-century Christmas card

3.39 Late nineteenth-century Christmas card

Christmas cards of that decade were essentially an idea that had not yet found its time; it was not until the 1860s that, building upon the practice of Christmas visitors writing greetings on and embellishing their visiting cards, printers began to produce Christmas cards in considerable numbers.

The introduction in 1870 of the ½d stamp for postcards gave a boost to the Christmas card trade, but the practice of sending cards was confined to the upper and middle classes until the 1880s, when manufacturers began producing cheaper cards for as little as a few pence a dozen. Thereafter the sending of cards spread to most sections of society. As *The Times* declared in 1883:

> This wholesome custom has been ... frequently the happy means of ending strifes, cementing broken friendships and strengthening family and neighbourhood ties in all conditions of life. In this respect the Christmas card undoubtedly fulfils a high end, for cheap postage has constituted it almost exclusively the modern method of conveying Christmas wishes, and the increasing popularity of the custom is for this reason, if no other, a matter for congratulation.

Having been sent a Christmas card one was under some obligation to return the gesture, and by the 1890s the Post Office was finding difficulty in coping with the annual bulge in its mail.

Many Christmas cards have been of high aesthetic merit and can be considered part of the history of art and design; such leading illustrators as Kate Greenaway (see Plate I), Walter Crane and Randolph Caldecott were active in this field in the 1870s and '8os and firms like Tuck and Son, De La Rue and Marcus Ward in Britain, and Prang's of Boston in the United States, competed for the best designers. From the beginning only a minority of cards depicted the Nativity and the main symbols were those relating to the popular or folk aspects of Christmas: mistletoe, plum puddings, robins, holly and Father Christmas. Many of the early cards had comic themes which, like much nineteenth-century humour, can appear bizarre, vulgar or obscure to us. There were Christms cards featuring devils, insects, monsters and rats; there were some where the humour appears cruel and insensitive, with birds about to be caught by cats, for example; and a sub-genre portraying erotic studies of naked or scantily clad females, often very young girls.

The most important figure in the new Christmas which developed in the mid-nineteenth century was undoubtedly Father Christmas or Santa Claus. Every European society had, as we have seen, some legend of a spirit or personification of Christmas, legends which were almost certainly part of the southern European Saturnalia or the Yuletide of the Teutonic north before they took on a Christmas guise. The Christian tradition had adopted St Nicholas and each European country interpreted him and his seasonal visitations somewhat differently. With the Reformation, England and Scotland turned their backs on St Nicholas, and the English Father Christmas of the seventeenth and eighteenth centuries, or Old Christmas, Sir Christmas or Captain Christmas as he was variously known, was a somewhat Saturnalian version of the spirit of festivity. In some depictions he was a rather impish Lord of Misrule holding a glass in his hand, while in others he was lean and gaunt and more akin to Old Father Time.

The American Santa Claus is, of course, based upon the Dutch St Nicholas or Santa Klaus. In accordance with Dutch custom the children of immigrants in New York State would put out their shoes on St Nicholas's Eve (St Nicholas's Day was 6 December) hoping that they would be filled by Santa Claus. The custom spread beyond the descendants of Dutch immigrants and was transferred to Christmas Eve. The modern Santa Claus, however, emerged almost complete in the 1820s from the pen of one man, Professor Clement Clark Moore, of New York State. His poem *A Visit From St Nicholas* – often known as *The Night Before Christmas* – was published anonymously in 1823 in the *Troy Sentinel*, a local newspaper, and immediately became wildly popular. Moore's creation of Santa Claus may well have drawn upon Washington Irving's *Knickerbocker's History of New York* (1809) which provided similar information about Santa Claus's visit; and an 1821 issue of *The Children's Friend*, published in New York City, had portrayed the visitor as travelling by a sleigh drawn by reindeer – but it was Moore who made popular what has become the standard image of Santa Claus. The New York professor would no doubt have preferred to be remembered for his Hebrew lexicon, his translation of Juvenal or his many other poems rather than for a light work written to entertain his own children

and published without his consent, but he is now known only as the man who invented Santa Claus.

Moore described a Santa Claus who arrived on a sledge drawn by flying reindeer on Christmas Eve; he came down the chimney with his sack of gifts, he filled the stockings of children; and he was merry and rubicund:

> His eyes how they twinkled! His dimples how merry!
> His cheeks were like roses, his nose like a cherry.
>
> His droll little mouth was drawn up like a bow
> And the beard on his chin was as white as the snow.

I   Kate Greenaway (1846-1901): *Illustrated London News* cover, Christmas Number 1880.

II   Robert Braithwaite Martineau (1826-69): 'The Christmas
Hamper' (The Bridgeman Art Gallery).

III   Henry J. Jones: 'The Uxbridge Coach' (The Bridgeman Art Gallery)

IV   'The Squire's Christmas Box' *Graphic,*
Christmas Number 1887.

V   'Errand of Charity' *Graphic,* Christmas Number 1880.

VI   *Illustrated London News* cover, Christmas Number 1897.

VII   G. E. Studdy: 'Hallo Santa!' *Blackie's Children's Annual* 1922
(Mary Evans Picture Library).

VIII   Harrods interiors,
Christmas 1985 (Dr Milo Shott).

IX Regent Street, London, illuminations, Christmas 1981
(Dr Milo Shott).

X Manchester Town Hall, Christmas 1984 (Dr Colin Cunningham).

XI Washington Irving's home, 'Sleepy Hollow', Tarrytown, NY. Each year the house is opened for the public to participate in a 'traditional' American Christmas (Anne McGregor).

XII Christmas in the millionaires' mansions of Newport, Rhode Island (The Preservation Society of Newport County).
a. Chateau-sur-Mer: dining room
b. Marble House: poinsettia tree.

The stump of a pipe he held tight in his teeth,
And the smoke, it encircled his head like a wreath.

He had a broad face and a little round belly
That shook, when he laughed, like a bowl full of jelly.

He was chubby and plump, a right jolly old elf,
And I laughed when I saw him, in spite of myself.

It was left to Thomas Nast, the illustrator, to fix the physical appearance of Santa Claus. His earlier drawings for *Harper's Weekly*, which he began in 1863, show the Christmas visitor as resembling Moore's 'jolly old elf' but in his later work he settled on the portrayal which has become definitive: a large, jovial, white-bearded figure dressed in a red suit with white fur trimmings and a matching cap.

Santa Claus swept aside all rivals, such as the German Pelz-Nickel and Kriss Kringle (the Christkind), in America and he rapidly imposed his personality and customs upon the English Father Christmas. The names Father Christmas and Santa Claus became interchangeable in Britain although English artists

3.40 An 'old' depiction of Father Christmas: W.J. Linton's illustration of a hedonistic Father Christmas. *Illustrated London News*, 28 December 1847

3.41 Another 'old' Father Christmas: this time he is 'lean and gaunt and rather akin to Old Father Time'. *Illustrated London News*, 23 December 1848

3.43 'Caught!' Nast
produced many sentimental
drawings of Santa Claus

depicted him in a red habit with a hood rather than the red suit and cap
favoured in America. The new Santa Claus/Father Christmas was in fact an
amalgam of the American, Dutch and English traditions. The custom of his
bringing presents to children came from the Dutch legend but, whereas in that
tradition he had been an ascetic saint on a grey horse, Moore drew on the old
Christmas of England for the jovial character and appearance of his creation.
Indeed, if Santa Claus was part St Nicholas and part a Father Christmas
descended from the Lord of Misrule, with antecedents going further back to
Saturnalia, the latter characteristics were the more prominent. It is significant
that Moore failed to mention the Nativity in his poem; Santa Claus was a fitting
figure to preside over a modern Saturnalia, the Saturnalia of an increasingly
urbanised, humanitarian, family-centred and child-loving civilisation. Within
a few decades this kindly and merry figure had been established without any
great publicity or controversy at the very heart of the emerging Anglo-
American Christmas.

3.42 (opposite) Thomas Nast
created the physical
appearance of Santa Claus
which has been copied to this
day

The old twelve day season of Christmas had, as we have seen, become moribund by the late eighteenth century and for many Christmas Day itself had become an ordinary working day. The Victorian period saw a reversal of the tendency to curtail holidays and from 1834 Christmas Day was one of the few days officially recognised as a holiday. This concentration on Christmas Day was not universally popular at first and some workers insisted on taking their customary New Year's Day holiday in lieu of Christmas Day. Gradually, however, in most parts of England, although not in Scotland, Christmas Day became the major holiday. From the 1860s there was a growing tendency to switch present giving from New Year to Christmas Day. Then, in England, the Bank Holiday Act of 1871 gave formal recognition to the growing practice of extending the holiday to include Boxing Day. Boxing Day, said *The Times* on this occasion, was 'the Saturnalia of our people, secured to it now by Act of Parliament'. It remained the day for giving gifts to tradesmen, but Twelfth Night cakes followed the trend of centring nearly everything upon the one big day and became Christmas cakes, imposing yet another challenge to the digestive system upon Christmas Day.

The federal structure of the United States meant that the increasing popularity of Christmas was followed by the gradual recognition, state by state, of Christmas Day as a public holiday – Alabama recognised Christmas Day in 1836 and Oklahoma in 1890 but between 1845 and 1865 no less than 28 states accorded legal recognition to the holiday.

3.44 Christmas shopping: 'Returning home with the spoils'. *Illustrated London News*, 25 December 1876

3.45 (opposite) It was recognised very early on that Christmas could be a costly time: 'The costs of Christmas'. *Illustrated London News*, 24 December 1853

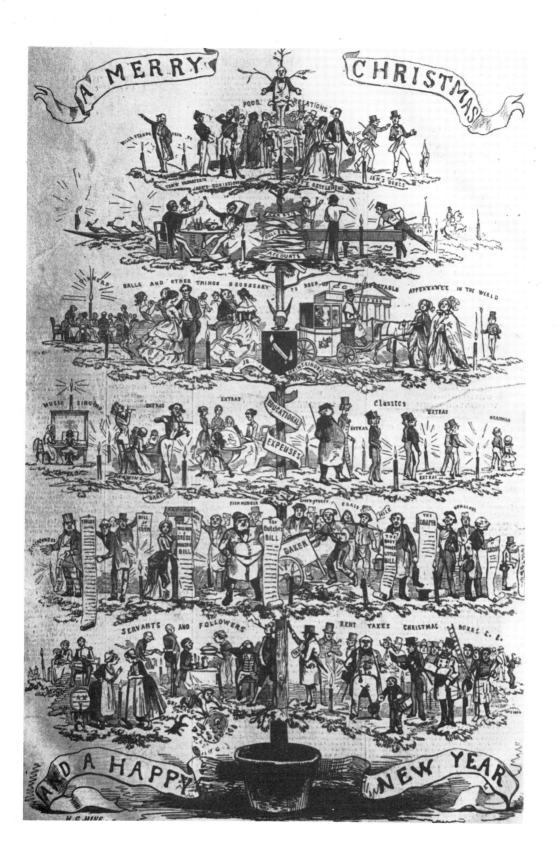

By the late nineteenth century the modern Christmas had settled into the pattern we know today. The season began with a period of anticipation and preparation in which Christmas shopping became increasingly more important; earlier in the century the main Christmas expenditure had been on food and drink but, as the custom of giving presents to children, other relations and friends became more popular, shopping became part of the ritual of Christmas, a ritual enthusiastically endorsed by the retail trade which responded with advertisements and gaily decorated stores. The cards were written and posted, the tree set up and decorated, the presents wrapped and the ubiquitous turkey, which was fast replacing the goose or the baron of beef, prepared. Then came family reunions, the visit of Santa Claus, the singing of carols and preliminary incursions into the Christmas fare. On Christmas Day itself the children played with their newly acquired toys, adults exchanged presents and then came the ceremonious Christmas dinner, pre-eminently a family occasion but, in army barracks or ships at sea, and even in the workhouse, the hallowed right of every man and woman.

3.46 'Returning from church'. *Illustrated London News*, Christmas Supplement 1855

3.47 Victorians were intrigued by the thought of Christmas abroad, especially the notion of Christmas in summer: 'Christmas in the Jungle'. *Illustrated London News*, Christmas 1878

3.48 'Christmas in Australia'.
Illustrated London News,
Christmas Number 1881

Significantly, it was only the singing of carols that had a peculiarly religious significance. Attendance at a church service was not for the majority an inseparable accompaniment to Christmas. The Victorian period in both Britain and America was a time of deep and sincere religiosity so that it is something of a paradox that it should have seen the development of a folk Christmas that was secular if not pagan in inspiration and character. The churches followed rather than led the new popular Christmas. Fundamentalist sects continued to ignore the 'pagan festival' but most churches encouraged the celebration of Christmas. For many, especially among the middle classes, the religious message of Christmas was important and church going on Christmas Day essential, but for most working people Christianity provided the colouring rather than the essence of the festival. Yet the modern Anglo-American Christmas was more than just a cosy feast of urban societies no longer subjected to the mid-winter hardships that inspired the original Saturnalia or Yuletide, though it was that in part. The late Victorian Christmas had a spiritual significance but it was less a Christian spirituality than one which drew upon the warm but sentimental humanitarianism epitomised by Charles Dickens; it saluted and celebrated the family, childhood and the extended family of the nation.

FOUR

Christmas in the Twentieth Century

By 1900 Christmas was *the* holiday in both Britain and the United States. Most of the main characteristics of the modern Christmas had been established but it was a very different festival from the one which the early Victorians had remembered and envied. Mumming and guising were little more than folk memories save in some country districts, while many of the special seasonal foods and drinks which had enjoyed great regional variations had almost disappeared. The new Christmas in Britain and America was more standardised and more national.

As such an emphasis is placed upon tradition at Christmas time, it is at first

4.1 At the end of the century Christmas was still being set in a past age. Note the clothing worn by the children

4.2 There was a time when trains ran on Christmas Day: 'Christmas Day in a Signal Box – Father's Dinner'. *Illustrated London News*, 1895

sight surprising that in the United States, where a stream of immigrants brought their own customs with them, we should be able to talk of an American Christmas. As we have seen, the English tradition did merge with other influences and many of the resultant customs were then re-exported to England. Yet the twentieth century has seen the increasing dominance of a Christmas which is essentially Anglo-Saxon, or more accurately Anglo-American. This can most clearly be seen in the emphasis upon Christmas Day as the time for opening the gifts from Santa Claus, the exchange of gifts and the important celebratory meal. Of course, one can find families or even regions where German, Italian or Scandinavian traditions are cherished in a pristine state, and many more where special foods or decorations testify to ethnic origins, but overall the tendency, especially of later immigrants, has been to adapt to the national American Christmas. Such a process has undoubtedly been assisted by the media, by service in the armed forces and by commercial pressures. More profoundly, Christmas has been, like the English language and the Constitution of the United States, part of the machinery of Americanisation.

Since 1900 there has been a vast increase in the observance of the Christmas festival. The preparations for Christmas start even earlier, the holiday is longer and the pressures to buy an ever-widening choice of presents, food and drink are more intense. For some, Christmas has become a full-time occupation. There are many industries and, indeed, even shops, which are entirely devoted to the Christmas trade. Most ordinary retail stores stock up with Christmas goods some three or four months in advance and Father Christmases start to appear in department stores from October onwards. Much larger quantities of food and drink and cards and presents are bought than eighty years ago. Nowadays, over twice the quantity of wines and spirits is bought in the period from October to December compared with any other quarter of the year, and whereas around five million letters and cards were sent through the post in Britain in the 1880s, by the early 1980s this had risen to over 1,000 million. In the United States, Christmas cards are even more popular and on average twice as many cards are bought per person than in Britain.

It would be easy to reel off a string of statistics demonstrating just how commercialised Christmas has become compared with one hundred years ago, but the more interesting and significant feature of the twentieth-century Christmas is not so much its burgeoning commercialisation but rather how many Victorian Christmas values have been preserved and, in some instances, actually reinforced. The idea of Christmas as a time when the poor, lonely and unfortunate should be especially remembered has continued, while the emphasis on the home, family and Christmas as a time for indulging children has been strengthened even further.

As we have seen in the previous chapter, these ideals were fairly firmly embedded in late nineteenth-century society. Studies of the English working class in the period before the First World War show that Christmas was the most important date in the calendar, even more so than birthdays, and that even in low income families efforts were made to decorate houses and obtain presents for children. But as the twentieth century has progressed, there has been a greater emphasis on nostalgia, home, family and children. An Opinion Research Centre survey in Britain in 1972 concluded that not only did the majority of those questioned consider Christmas as essentially a family occasion, but that

4.3 Heaney & Co. Fish & Fruit dealers, 44 Fishergate, Preston c.1902

4.4 Harrods Meat Hall, Christmas 1929

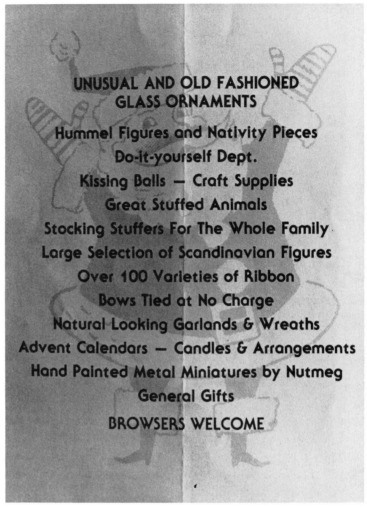
4.5 The Silver Skate Shop: a shop devoted entirely to the Christmas trade

4.6 An advertisement for the Silver Skate Shop

4.7 Santa's workshop, North Pole, Colorado

4.8 A Christmas cracker factory – part of the burgeoning Christmas industry. The modern cracker with its loud bang was developed in Britain in the Victorian period

the level of response to this question was similar for all age groups, social classes and regions of the country.

For some of the very poor, Christmas in the early twentieth-century was largely a time for charitable hand-outs. Richard Morgan, who came from a one-parent family, recalled that by attending the local Ragged School regularly, he was rewarded by being allowed to queue up at the school on Christmas morning for a meat pie, a mince pie, a ham sandwich and a cup of tea. However, when working through oral histories for the early years of the century, the extent to which most speakers associate Christmas with home and the family is very marked. Frank Benson, the son of a skilled iron moulder working in a textile factory in Bolton, recalled that the children received presents of dolls, toys and sweets and that

We always had a good Christmas dinner. A joint of pork or a fowl. In the afternoon Aunties and Uncles would come in for high tea and we'd have a party after tea and games and everybody would generally let their hair down, and have a jolly evening.

Gwen Davis, who was one of seven children from a working class family living

84

ONE·OF·THE
WORKROOMS

However dark the wintry night may be
May Gladness light it like a Christmas tree.

in Port Talbot, remembered Christmas as a time of

> ... a big tea, tarts, trifles, everything else and, all the crowd, the house was always packed. And then there was music in the front room, singing, hymns, carols – it was quite a day. And Boxing Day. We had two wonderful days ... It was always open door.
>
> (quoted in Paul Thompson, *The Edwardians*)

For poorer families Christmas was often a quieter affair. Fred Mills, one of twelve children of a farm labourer in Essex, recalled that he might receive

4.10 Christmas card, 1984: the subject matter hasn't changed very much

presents of oranges and nuts from relations at Christmas time, but that although his family was friendly with the neighbours in the village, 'like many poor families they had not the resources to invite them in'. Most people had expectations of how Christmas should be spent and when these expectations were not fulfilled Christmas could become one of the loneliest and saddest days of the year. A woman in service in Lancashire in the 1900s remembered:

> One Christmas I was at Longbridge and Christmas Day come and I was a bit homesick, you know, and had our Christmas Day's dinner. I washed up and all that, and she said 'Has tha finished now?' I said 'Yes madam' so she said, 'Well if thou get all the paper there, you'll see a lot of paper there and there's a big needle there and a ball of string, if you go down to the paddock (that was the toilet) sit there and take the scissors and cut some paper up and thread it for the lavatory.' And I sat there on Christmas Day and I think I cried a bucketful of tears. Christmas afternoon and I was sat . . . sitting cutting bits of paper like that . . . till about half past four when I went in for m'tea. Sitting there on the lavatory seat.
> (quoted in Elizabeth Roberts, *A Woman's Place*)

The major difference between many early twentieth century Christmases and those of the present day is that, generally speaking, modern family gatherings are smaller and concern the immediate family rather than involving numerous branches of it. In one sense this is not surprising. After all, as a result of higher living standards and birth control, family sizes are smaller. In both Britain and America, the average size of families in all classes has declined since 1900, and whereas the average number of children in a British family in 1900 was 3.4, now it is under 2.

Partly because families are now smaller, there is even more pressure put on each family to ensure that none of their nearest and dearest spend the day on their own. So, many people feel that they have very little choice in deciding how they will spend Christmas. Arrangements are made, either for elderly parents to visit their children, or for young families to visit grandma and grandpa over Christmas. In the days preceding Christmas Day, roads, trains, coaches and airlines are crowded with people undertaking journeys, most of which are connected with visits to their families. A British National Travel survey compiled just over ten years ago discovered that in December, of those people who spent nights away from home, 75% were spending them with members of their family.

Another outcome of the smaller family Christmas is that more time can be devoted by parents to children. This can be trying and exhausting but very few would, even if secretly admiring Evelyn Waugh's actions, do what he did at Christmas 1945. As he recorded in his diary, 'By keeping the children in bed for long periods we managed to have a tolerable day ... The children leave for Pixton on the 10th. Meanwhile I have my meals in the library.'

Despite Waugh and his sympathisers, children have become increasingly the focus of Christmas Day festivities. Here, of course, parents are confronted with enormous commercial pressures. TV, newspaper and magazine advertising ensure the children themselves are fully aware of the toys and games available in most shops and, in a survey conducted for IPC magazines in 1973, it was discovered that well over half the total number of all presents bought in Britain were intended for children.

The growing importance of the child-orientated aspects of Christmas, in societies which have been permissive in their treatment of children, is evidenced by the way in which Santa Claus has become almost the dominant symbol of the festival. As we have seen, the nineteenth-century Santa Claus was refashioned from the remnants of a variety of traditions, some secular and some religious; he became the embodiment of joy and merriment as well as an expression of affection for and devotion to children. In the twentieth century these latter characteristics have become even more pronounced. The older Germanic tradition that the seasonal visitor rewarded good children *and* punished the bad is long gone. Few would now have the heart to fill the stocking of the recalcitrant child with cinders! All children, it is felt, have a right to a rewarding visit from Santa.

Indeed, if the newspapers or television stations wish to tug the heart-strings in the interests of a charitable cause or a hard-luck story, Santa Claus rather than the infant Christ is likely to be invoked. A headline such as 'Ethiopian children will be without Santa this Christmas' is guaranteed to bring in a stream of donations.

Commercial interests have found Santa Claus as useful as have charities: he is not only used widely to sell goods and services, but since the 1920s it has become conventional for department stores to install 'real' Santas. The *New York Times* commented in 1927:

> A standardised Santa Claus appears to New York children – height, weight, stature are almost exactly standardised, as are the red garments, the hood and the white whiskers. The pack full of toys, ruddy cheeks and nose, bushy eyebrows and a jolly, paunchy effect are also inevitable parts of the requisite make-up.

Children obviously become confused when they are confronted by a Santa at every street corner, the same beaming figure in his Grotto at the department store and yet another look-alike at a Christmas party, yet their faith generally endures until an elder brother or the 'big boy of the block' disillusions them. It is the adults who are made most miserable by the inevitable exposure of the myth. Judge John H. Hatcher of the West Virginia Supreme Court even brought the law to the defence of Santa Claus with his opinion 'Ex parte Santa Claus' in 1927:

> Let legislators outlaw the law of evolution, if they must; let the Constitution be amended till it looks like a patch-work quilt; but rob not childhood of its most intriguing mystery – Santa Claus. Let him be to succeeding generations as he has been to us – a joyous faith of childhood, a pleasant indulgence of parenthood and a happy memory of old age.

Newspapers and magazines, as well as all the media new to the twentieth century, have benefited from the commercial opportunities provided by the Christmas festival and all, in their turn and in their different ways, have put a greater emphasis on the celebration of Christmas. Perhaps surprisingly, however, instead of promoting a wider variety of activities for people, they have all concentrated on making the observance of Christmas Day an even more uniform habit, not merely in the sense of Christmas being recognised as a special

4.11 'Santa Claus's Rebuke' by Thomas Nast. This drawing, subtitled 'I'll never do it again' reminds us that Santa Claus is only supposed to bring presents to *good* children. Yet, the viewer is led to believe that Nast's jolly elf will produce a present after delivering his rebuke

4.12 Christmas shopping 1923: even then shoppers were being urged to use the London tube during the non-peak period

holiday, but in the sense of how the day itself is spent. The reasons why this has come about are complex, but all the media have tended to reinforce the familiarity of the old rituals rather than developing new ones.

Newspapers and magazines have, despite technological advances, changed very little in the sentiments they express about Christmas since the nineteenth century. The famous *Saturday Evening Post* Christmas covers, especially those of the 1920s and 1930s, are proof of this. J.C. Leyendecker's drawings very often depicted a Christmas past with characters clothed either in medieval or early nineteenth-century costumes. Many of Norman Rockwell's illustrations for the same magazine were of Victorian Christmas scenes, if not of Mr Pickwick himself, and when he was not stressing the nostalgia of Christmas, Rockwell was emphasizing the season as a time particularly for children, with Santa Claus plotting his course around the world in order to visit all the 'extra good boys and girls.'

Today newspapers and magazines are still putting the emphasis firmly on Christmas as a family festival, but the family is depicted in a particular way and the values that are ascribed to it are those belonging to the 'traditional family'.

4.13 Children enjoying the Harrods toy fair, Christmas 1932

4.14 Special advertising for Christmas, 1939

Glynis Johns is giving her father, Mervyn Johns, a Parker '51' for Christmas

new Parker '51'

The world's most wanted pen

I'M SENDING CHESTERFIELDS to all my friends.
That's the merriest Christmas any smoker can have —
Chesterfield mildness plus no unpleasant after-taste

Ronald Reagan

CHESTERFIELD *"Buy the beautiful "Christmas-card" carton*

4.15 The use of film stars to endorse Christmas gifts, 1955

4.16 The famous Chesterfield Christmas advertisement, 1952

4.17 *Saturday Evening Post* cover designed by J.C. Leyendecker, 23 December 1933 (The Curtis Publishing Co.)

4.18 Norman Rockwell's 'Extra Good Boys and Girls'. *Saturday Evening Post*, 16 December 1939 (Estate of Norman Rockwell)

THE SATURDAY EVENING POST

Dec. 23, '33

RIGHT-HO, JEEVES—By P. G. WODEHOUSE

4.19 'It's that special time of the year when being part of a family means so much ... more to the Queen, perhaps, than to most of us.' *Woman's Realm*, 22/29 December 1979

In Christmas editions articles abound on the subject of how the famous, particularly TV and film stars, will be spending their Christmas Day and, invariably, the vast majority of those questioned maintain they will be having a 'traditional' Christmas with their family in front of the hearth and participating in Christmas rituals such as dinner, crackers and party games. Typical of many is the article in *Woman's Realm* of 22/29 December 1979 entitled 'Christmas in the Castle'. In the course of the article we learn that Christmas 'is the only time of the year when the 24 or so members of the inner Royal Family circle can forget their responsibilities and the commitments demanded by their position, and relax together.' We are told about how the family spend Christmas Day itself. In the morning they attend a church service:

> The service is a traditional one – similar to those which take place in every parish church in the land – with carols, candles and decorations.
>
> After the service, the family go home for lunch. Like many of her subjects, the Queen likes it to be traditional but informal. Turkey, plum pudding with brandy sauce, and mince pies are on the menu. And there are crackers filled with jokes, trinkets and paper hats to keep the youngsters happy.

At one and the same time the Royal Family is portrayed both as something special and as a family which values the Christmas festival in much the same way as do most other families in the land.

4.20 Concentration on the Royal Family at Christmas: Edward, Prince of Wales at a Christmas Party 1922

At the same time that the 'traditional family' Christmas is put forward as the ideal Christmas, so those who are unfortunate or who are homeless at Christmas are particularly remembered. As poverty, hardship and loneliness are states which, unfortunately, are ever-present in our society, so articles and leaders on the subject change very little from year to year. *The Times* account, on Christmas Eve 1984, of the plans of Crisis at Christmas to provide temporary shelter and food for about 1,000 people in London over the six day Christmas period, is very similar to those reports in its nineteenth-century editions concerning the efforts of charitable institutions in towns and cities at Christmas time.

Just as newspapers and magazines play their part in sponsoring and helping Christmas charities, so too the cinema, especially in its heyday in the 1930s, has involved itself in charitable enterprises at Christmas. The cynic, with much justification, may well claim that cinema managers and distributors were not entirely uninterested parties in this respect, and that a medium which depended very much on the attendance of working class people and the poorer sections of society, would not lose out by being beneficent at Christmas time. Certainly, many cinemas ran schemes similar to those of the Ragged Schools mentioned earlier in the chapter, whereby if a child had 52 marks on his cinema card (this signified 52 visits to the cinema during the course of the year) the child was entitled to attend a free Christmas show. Other cinemas in the 1930s put on, through the efforts of cinema managers and local tradesmen, Christmas shows for the young and unemployed. In Sheffield in 1930, for example, the 'Regent' and 'Albert Hall' cinemas were the venues for Christmas morning performances for 4,500 of the poorest children in the area. All the children were given presents of toys at the end of the show. Again, in the same year in Salford, Victorian methods were resorted to in the selection of children for the Christmas cinema show, and local patrons, clergy, magistrates and doctors were asked to recommend deserving children. Sometimes the attention given to children went beyond a film performance and a toy. At some cinemas doctors and nurses would be in attendance and the children were given medical examinations as they queued for the start of the film.

In the 1930s a free film show was one of the most popular methods of providing the poor and unfortunate with Christmas entertainment. Even in British jails films were shown on Christmas Day, although the prison authorities, just as their Victorian predecessors would have done, insisted that the films be of an improving nature. However, this stern policy was broken in 1937 when, instead of the usual cultural and educational films, *Boys Will Be Boys* featuring Will Hay was shown to 350 long-term convicts at Maidstone Prison.

In its depiction of Christmas, the film industry has followed traditional lines. Just as *A Christmas Carol* was quickly transferred from the book to the stage, so there have been numerous film versions made of the story both in Britain and the United States. A British silent version in 1908 was followed by an American one in 1910; since then there have been a number of talkies and, in 1970, a technicolour panavision musical version starring Albert Finney.

Only very occasionally has the cinema industry gone outside Dickens for Christmas stories. The most recent example is *Santa Claus – The Movie*, starring

4.21 *A Christmas Carol* adapted for the cinema: the 1935 production of *Scrooge*. Donald Calthorp as Cratchit celebrating Christmas with his family (National Film Archive London)

4.22 Another version of *A Christmas Carol* made in the United States in 1938: the reformed Scrooge, played by Reginald Owen, has showered gifts on Tiny Tim (Tony Kilburn). (National Film Archive London)

4.23 The 1970 musical version of *Scrooge*: Albert Finney as Scrooge goes singing down a London street (National Film Archive London)

4.24 A sceptical young
Natalie Wood pulls Santa
Claus's beard (Edmund
Gwenn) while a bored John
Payne looks on: scene from
Miracle on 34th Street
(National Film Archive
London)

Dudley Moore (Disney studios have in production at present *Father Christmas*)
but the most interesting movie of this kind was *Miracle on 34th Street* made in 1947.
The film won an Oscar for Edmund Gwenn who played the part of Kris Kringle,
an old gentleman who was convinced he was Santa Claus. After being turned
out of a mental institution, Kringle obtains employment as Santa Claus at
Macy's department store on 34th Street. Through a mixture of genuine honesty
and a naivety in dealing with customers, which includes suggesting that they
purchase goods from other stores, Kringle brings back the spirit of Christmas
into the hearts of hardened businessmen and a sceptical child. Although the film
is nearly forty years old, its story is still remembered and Macy's advertising
publicity for Christmas 1984 included the headline, 'The Miracle of 34th Street
is happening again.'

Generally speaking, however, Christmas has figured in films as an incident in
storylines rather than as a central feature. In this respect the cinema has
followed the stage in often using Christmas as a dramatic device for underlining
the unity or the division within a family. In fact, it is a safe bet for cinemagoers to
assume that very shortly after seeing scenes of snow and houses decorated with
holly, they will be witnessing either a family celebration or a family tragedy.

The most popular Christmas films have been *Holiday Inn* (1942), starring Bing
Crosby and Fred Astaire, and *White Christmas* (1954), this time featuring Bing
Crosby and Danny Kaye. *White Christmas* was essentially a re-vamp of the
Holiday Inn story and was the top box-office film in both Canada and the United

States in 1954. It still remains in the top ten of the most financially successful musical films ever made. Both films had musical scores written by Irving Berlin and in both Bing Crosby sang 'White Christmas'. Berlin was awarded an Oscar for the song in 1942 and it was to become not only the most popular of Christmas songs but the biggest money-spinning popular song of all time. The copyright of 'White Christmas' still remains the most valuable song property in the world.

Another enormously successful Christmas song was 'Rudolph the Red-Nosed Reindeer' composed by Jonny Marks in 1949. In this instance, Marks was able to utilise a short story by Robert L. May written ten years earlier. Song and story together constitute one of the few enduring additions of the twentieth century to Christmas legend. It is the standard story of the under-dog, or in this case 'under-deer', who makes good. The butt of jokes among his reindeer companions because of his shiny red nose, Rudolph triumphs one Christmas Eve when the sky is overcast and the shiny nose enables Santa and his reindeer team to deliver presents and return safely to the North Pole. Rudolph has now joined Clement Moore's reindeer creations as a permanent member of Santa's team.

Most Christmas songs are, however, ephemeral and the majority are also celebrations of a secular or folk Christmas rather than of the religious festival. Harry Belafonte's 'Mary's boy child' is an exception to this, a popular yet religious song which has almost established itself as a carol. Each year record companies search for a new Christmas song which will be a commercial success with the record-buying public. Christmas 1984 saw a variaton of this when a

4.25 The traditional Christmas dinner is brought in to a young-looking Bing Crosby: a scene from *Holiday Inn* (National Film Archive London)

4.26 A rather embarrassed-looking Bing Crosby on the set of *White Christmas* (National Film Archive London)

4.27 1926: An early advertisement for 'wireless sets'

4.28 The 1925 Christmas number of *Radio Times* (BBC Enterprises)

large number of British pop stars got together to produce 'Do they know it's Christmas'. The song was top of the British hit parade for many weeks and all proceeds went to the Band Aid Ethiopian relief fund.

Film distributors now take great care to ensure that there is a top selection of family films on show in the cinemas during Christmas week. This was not always the case. In the 1930s and '40s, when the cinema was the major leisure entertainment, and cinema ticket sales rose even higher during Christmas week, cinema distributors had no difficulty in wooing potential customers. As a Mr Harrison wrote in his diary after a visit to the local Ritz cinema on Christmas Day 1939, 'It was a third rate film chosen for Xmas as everyone would go no matter what was on'. However, the major Christmas attraction nowadays for families is not the films being shown in the cinemas but the films being screened by the television companies.

First radio, and then television, unlike the cinema, have reinforced the

tendency for Christmas to be a festival celebrated behind closed doors – a phenomenon which a walk through any suburban housing estate at midday on Christmas Day will confirm. Radio, the novelty of the '20s, and the established focus of entertainment in the '30s, was influential in keeping families in at least geographical proximity to each other. The importance of Christmas to the BBC is reflected in the fact that over one million copies of the Christmas edition of the *Radio Times* was sold as early as 1927.

Both radio and television have enabled national leaders to talk to entire populations. It is significant that they have tended to do so at Christmas time and that they have emphasized that they are talking to families. On Christmas

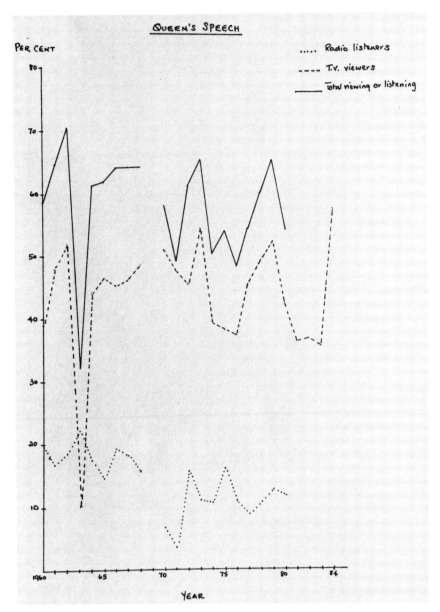

QUEEN'S SPEECH

PER CENT

..... Radio listeners

- - - - T.V. viewers

———— Total viewing or listening

YEAR

4.30 Percentage of the population watching or listening to the Queen's speech on Christmas Day (*BBC Audience Research survey*). Figures dropped alarmingly in 1963, primarily because BBC TV transmitted the speech at 9.30 a.m. instead of the usual after dinner slot of 3 p.m. In 1969 it was decided not to broadcast the speech but there were so many protests that the broadcasts were resumed the following year. From these figures one can see that on average some 50–60% of the population listen to or watch the Queen's broadcast

Day 1932 King George V made a broadcast which was transmitted throughout the British Empire. The speech was deliberately designed to convey a fatherly tone – the King addressing his extended family, the Empire. The broadcast was a great success and became an annual event carried on by successive monarchs.

Very rarely have the Christmas talks not touched at some point on the theme of the family. In 1952 Elizabeth II stated that 'At Christmas our thoughts are always full of our homes and our families. It is the day when members of the same family try to come together or, if separated by distance or events, meet in spirit and affection by exchanging greetings'. Two years later the Queen remarked that 'to all of us there is nothing quite like the family gathering in familiar surroundings, centred on the children whose festival this truly is, in the

4.31 Percentage of the population watching TV hourly on Christmas Day, 1984 (*BBC Audience Research survey*). Between 3 p.m. and 11 p.m. on Christmas Day over half the population had their television sets turned on and around 8 p.m. in the evening over 70% of the population were watching television

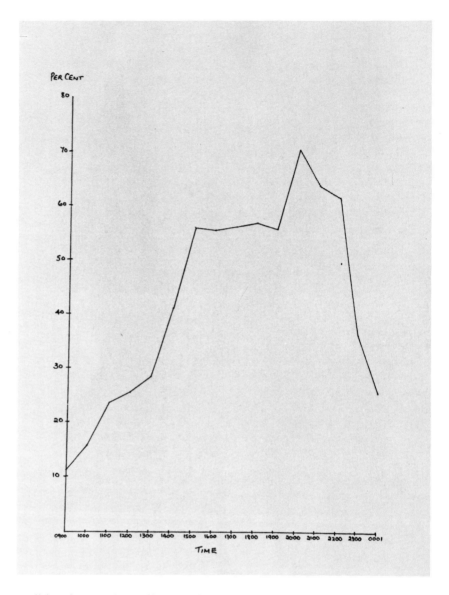

traditional atmosphere of love and happiness that springs from the enjoyment of simple, well tried things'.

That Christmas is seen as a unifying influence cementing not only family relationships but the greater 'family' of the nation, is also illustrated in the American 'traditions' which, like the Queen's speech, have come to represent the unity of the nation at Christmas time. The lighting ceremony for the Christmas tree at the White House was broadcast for the first time as early as 1925; the President's broadcast to the American nation parallels that of the Queen to the British; while the carol service on the White House lawn is also an annual institution.

For many, television is central to the entertainment of Christmas Day. Certainly, it is the Christmas pastime on which the newspapers concentrate. For example, the *Sun* newspaper in Britain in its Christmas Eve edition devoted about half of its space to television information and programmes. So, the 'traditional' Christmas now appears to be one which is spent with the family, where presents are distributed, especially to the children, a special dinner is consumed and then the television set is turned on. In one sense it seems remarkable that despite all the technological advances made in this century, and despite all the varied commercial pressures that are exerted in the months preceding Christmas, there is such a close similarity in the Christmas Day activities of so many people. Whereas we have little idea of how the majority of people in Britain were spending their time at 8pm on Christmas Day in 1884, we do know that at the same time one hundred years later, over 70% of the population were watching television and that of these nearly 20 million, or 37.5% of the population, were watching one film, *Raiders of the Lost Ark*.

Many of the unifying or standardising effects of television at Christmas may, however, prove to be a temporary phase, the result of a particular stage in the development of technology. Videos, cable TV, dishes and the plethora of TV channels may already be breaking up this concentration, a process which has gone far further in the United States. Instead of the united family gazing at the *Wizard of Oz*, individual members may be respectively watching baseball, a soap-opera, a newly issued film or a succession of pop videos in different rooms of the house.

One reason given for why the home has become an even more central feature of Christmas Day activities than in the nineteenth century, is that nowadays there are very few outdoor organised entertainments available on Christmas Day itself. Public transport is virtually non-existent and, apart from hotels and some restaurants being open, there is very little to tempt the public outside. This was not the case at the start of the century when newspapers were published and concerts, recitals, cinema shows and many sporting events took place on Christmas Day. Indeed, for a few, sporting activities took precedence over traditional Christmas rituals. George Ashworth, a soccer fanatic and a textile worker from Bacup in Lancashire, wrote in his diary on 25 December 1906:

> Went to Oswaldthistle this morning Bacup won 5–1. After match we went to Blackburn where we had dinner. After dinner went to see Blackburn R v Newcastle U. Blackburn Rovers 4–0 before a record gate which totalled 7,870, the highest ever taken at Blackburn for a League Match.

Gradually, however, the desire by all sections of the population to celebrate Christmas Day as a holiday, together with the later influence of television, meant that inevitably the number of Christmas Day activities was reduced. 1912 was the last year in which British daily newspapers were published on Christmas Day, and seven years later the young Evelyn Waugh commented on the lack of entertainment available. He wrote in his diary, 'Like birthdays, Christmas gets duller and duller. Soon it will merely be a day when the shops are inconveniently shut'. Nevertheless, there was still plenty to do outside the home on Christmas Day. Soccer, rugby league and rugby union matches, and greyhound racing meetings, all continued to take place on Christmas Day up until the outbreak of the Second World War and were resumed after it for a few years into the 1950s.

Even the number of church services on Christmas Day are fewer now than they were earlier in the century. Before 1914, Christmas morning and afternoon

4.32 Christmas Day football programme, 1937 (Chelsea F.C.): unfortunately the weather was not equal to the Christmas spirit and this game against Charlton Athletic was abandoned after 61 minutes owing to fog!

services were held in most parishes. But gradually, because of falling attendances, these services were reduced in number. It would be wrong, however, to assume that this drop in popularity was due to the growing secularisation of the Christmas festival. To a considerable extent carol services and midnight mass or communion services have, since the 1930s and particularly since the Second World War, supplanted services on Christmas Day itself. The 'holy night' had become the focus of religious feeling as the holy day has been given over to secular rejoicing. This development is both convenient, in that it leaves Christmas Day itself free for activities in the home, and can be justified on aesthetic and theological grounds: midnight services have an extra beauty as the faithful gather at an unusual hour in a candle-lit setting and the carol singing

and communal worship emphasise expectancy and the miracle of the birth. In the Church of England alone at Christmas 1982, nearly $1\frac{3}{4}$ million people attended Christmas night communion services. This is nearly three times the number of communicants on a normal Sunday and slightly more than the number who attend communion services on Easter Sunday.

Even if one is not religious, it is difficult not to be aware of the religious links with the Christmas festival. Many Christmas card firms continue to print cards which evoke the Nativity story, and school activities often involve carol concerts and Christmas plays. Indeed, one of the few innovations to Christmas festivities this century has been the reintroduction of the Nativity play. The ethos of Christianity is deeply embedded in the culture of both Britain and the United

4.34 Not only Christmas cards continue to depict scenes from the Nativity: Canadian postage stamp

4.35 Many countries now mark the season with special issues of stamps at Christmas: a US example

4.36 In 1981 in Britain a set of Christmas stamps was specially designed by young people

States. It extends to most art forms and aspects of education and so ensures that even if people do not subscribe to the Christmas story in a literal sense, the Christian setting remains a central aspect of Christmas.

Christmas exerts such a tremendous influence and imposes such a hiatus in the world of business and commerce that it is impossible for even sections of the population from non-Christian traditions to ignore it. Although the most orthodox of Jews ignore the festival, many other Jews have accepted the holiday as a general expression of 'goodwill towards men.' Many have adopted the Christmas tree custom and send cards without specifically Christian imagery. A recent development has been the printing of Hanukkah Calendars for Jewish children in conscious imitation of Advent Calendars.

Overall, the twentieth-century Christmas is not fundamentally different from that of the late nineteenth century. Many of the traditions – carols, Christmas cards and crackers – are just as popular if not more so. Even the pantomime, despite the closure of so many provincial theatres, continues to be a highlight of the Christmas season. Of course, there have been changes and innovations. The revival of Nativity plays has already been mentioned. The crib, which at the turn of the century was confined to Roman Catholic and a few Anglican churches, can now be seen not only in nearly all churches but also in department stores and numerous public buildings. Again, the Christmas tree is now not only placed in the home but appears in churches, shops and town squares. This is one of a number of instances in this century of Britain adopting customs originating in the United States. In 1912 a Christmas tree was placed for the first time in Madison Square, New York, but it was many years before a similar event occurred in a British town.

Undoubtedly the biggest change, apart from the influence of radio, television and video, has been the move back to the old pre-nineteenth-century idea of the celebration of the Twelve Days. An increasing number of people now enjoy an

4.37 Pantomime poster for *Mother Goose* at the Chelsea Palace, London, 1937

4.38 Christmas tree at the
Rockefeller Centre, New
York

4.39 Christmas tree and crib
at the Metropolitan Museum
of Art

4.40 Santa Claus keeps up
with technological changes:
on roller skates. *Punch*, 25
December 1875

4.41 ... and driving a car.
Punch, 26 December 1896

uninterrupted Christmas to New Year holiday. In 1984 in Britain most manufacturing industries closed down for a holiday of at least eleven days and it was only those involved in the retail and commercial sectors who had to return to work after Boxing Day. Apart from this, the old nineteenth-century ideals of charity, nostalgia, family and the home continue to be reinforced and predominant. In many ways Christmas habits and fashions and the people who celebrate them have changed surprisingly little.

4.42 Listening to the radio.
A 1929 Christmas card

A Merry Christmas

You're in my Christmas circuit
And on the waves of thought
A Happy Christmas and New Year
To you is gladly brought.

FIVE

Christmas in Wartime

In early December 1914, a few months after the start of the First World War, Pope Benedict XV put forward a proposal that all the warring armies should cease hostilities over the Christmas period. There were many reasons why this plan failed to be accepted but a very straightforward one was that the various powers involved would not have been able to agree on what constituted Christmas. The Pope clearly had in mind a period covering 25 December but members of the Christian Orthodox church celebrate Christmas Day thirteen days later and so would have found the 25th quite inappropriate. To put this in more general terms, most of us would see some justification, in time of war, for observing a truce on 25 December. After all, it is supposed to be a time of peace and goodwill to all men. Yet the same people would be much less inclined to observe a truce for a day early in January. In one sense this distinction is sheer nonsense. After all, what is the difference between attempting to kill an enemy on one particular day of the year rather than any other? Yet 25 December is such a significant date in the yearly calendar, even for non-practising Christians in Western Europe and the United States, that it demands different standards of behaviour from other times of the year.

A clear example of this can be seen during the closing stages of the American involvement in Vietnam. In May 1972 President Nixon, in an attempt finally to break the resistance of North Vietnam, declared: 'The bastards have never been bombed like they're to be bombed this time', and ordered massive air attacks on that country. Critics of the President strenuously attacked this policy, yet the outcry against him, not only in the United States but also in Western Europe, was nothing like that a few months later in December when, after summoning the Chairman of the Joint Chiefs of Staff and insisting, 'I don't want any more of this crap about the fact that we couldn't hit this target or that one,' President Nixon instituted the largest conventional bombing raids ever undertaken in any war. Undoubtedly, one reason why these 'Christmas bombings', as they came to be known, were so heavily criticised was that they were more intensive than those in May. Nevertheless, it is difficult to avoid the conclusion that another significant factor was that they took place at Christmas. Nixon's popularity rating in the United States fell to below 40% and Senator Aiken spoke for many when he condemned the raids and called them 'a sorry Christmas present'.

Christmas, then, is not only a special day in any calendar year, it takes on an added significance in times of war, when the values of Christmas appear to be challenged. Not only is the concept of peace and goodwill threatened but so too

Trusty Friends: "White Men" All of Them!

"AND HERE'S A HAND MY TRUSTY FIERE, AND GIE'S A HAND O' THINE——"
All round the world the familiar song has run, but never, and nowhere, have more tried and trusty friends clasped hands in the chorus than the comrades from all parts of the Empire who sang it with heart and voice in the trenches on the Christmas Day of 1915, surely the most momentous since Anno Domini One.

Robin Redbreast Calls on Our Lads in Khaki

"SAT ON THE END OF MY BAYONET LIKE A BLOOMIN' CHRISTMAS CARD, HE DID."—[Soldier's Letter.]

5.1 Soldiers from all parts of the Empire meet together in the trenches on Christmas Day: a morale-boosting illustration from *The War Illustrated*, Christmas 1915

5.2 Even in wartime the robin is used as a symbol of Christmas. *The War Illustrated*, Christmas 1915

is the main focus of the modern Christmas, the family unit. Different members of the family are constrained to be away from home by either fighting in the armed forces or helping in some other way with the war effort. What perhaps is remarkable is that in these limiting circumstances nations and families appear to make even greater efforts to celebrate the occasion, and that they attempt to observe it in as traditional a way as possible.

During the nineteenth century, however, the Christmas scenes depicted in newspapers and magazines at times of conflict, invariably concerned the men fighting on distant battlefronts rather than the wives and children back at home. Very often the war illustrations were of serving men dreaming of past Christmases spent together with their families, while maintaining guard against

5.3 Christmas Day in a battlefield. *Illustrated London News*, Christmas 1895

5.4 A poignant juxtaposition of the soldier thinking of home and the family awaiting his return (Thomas Nast)

5.5 One of the very many illustrations of soldiers at the battlefront dreaming of Christmas at home: 'Visions of a very different Christmas'. *The War Illustrated*, Christmas 1914

the enemy. Other popular illustrations were of soldiers relaxing and eating a make-shift but discernibly special Christmas dinner while taking time out from battle. Many of these drawings were unashamedly sentimental but others were published primarily in order to boost morale. This was certainly the aim behind Thomas Nast's drawing of Unionist soldiers relaxing during the Civil War. Not only were the soldiers of the Union celebrating but they were being visited by a Santa Claus, not in his usual garb, but in a uniform consisting of a star-spangled jacket and trousers striped like a flag. This device of appropriating Father Christmas and putting him firmly on your own side was soon copied in Britain. During the Afghan campaign of the late 1870s *The Graphic* printed an illustration containing various scenes of life at the front at Christmas, and one of the representations consisted of Father Christmas holding a rifle in the advance position and trampling over the words 'Peace' and 'Goodwill' which are written in the snow.

Perhaps this new, aggressive Father Christmas appealed to the jingoistic readers back home in Britain. The mood seems similar to that in Britain in 1914 when hundreds of thousands of men, in the first few months of the First World War, rushed to volunteer. It must have come as a surprise, therefore, to

Presents from Home: Good Cheer in the Dug-Out

CHRISTMAS EVE IN A CORNER OF NORTHERN FRANCE.

A hamper has arrived in Dug-Out Town, and the happy recipient "unloads." A turkey, sardines, cakes, and many other favourite edibles from home are displayed before eyes shining in anticipation of the coming feast.

newspaper and magazine editors when stories began filtering through at the end of December 1914 that at various sectors along a thirty mile stretch of the Western Front, many of the British and German troops had held an 'unofficial' Christmas 'truce'. So, although the Pope's proposals for a Christmas peace had sunk without trace, many officers and men participated in events which one commentator has called 'the best and most heartening Christmas story of modern times'.

Although the news of the 'truce' may have come as a surprise to those at home, for the more observant of the British High Command it was not totally unexpected. There had been a number of reports early in December 1914 of British and German troops calling and singing to each other across 'No Man's Land' and on one occasion there was a shooting match when opposing forces competed to hit a tin can set up mid way between the battle lines. This semi-fraternisation partly came about because after the heavy battles of October and November, the troops were now digging in, waiting for reinforcements, and realised that there was unlikely to be any general offensive for a few months. These circumstances, as General Sir Horace Smith-Dorrien, Commander of the Second Corps, noted in his diary, create the occasion when 'the greatest danger to the morale of troops exists' and he believed there was a great danger of 'troops becoming too friendly'. Indeed, Smith-Dorrien was so concerned that he sent out a directive to all his subordinate commanders urging them to keep up the

5.7 The same theme: Christmas Boxes in Camp during the American Civil War. A drawing by Winslow Homer for *Harper's Weekly* (Mary Evans Picture Library)

5.8 Thomas Nast's cartoon of Santa Claus visiting the Unionist army during the American Civil War

5.6 Troops at the front unpacking Christmas hampers. *The War Illustrated,* Christmas 1915

5.9 (opposite) 'The Afghan Campaign – Christmas tide at the Front'. Notice the aggressive Father Christmas in the inset towards the bottom of the picture. *Graphic*, 27 December 1879

5.10 Anti-German feelings remained strong throughout the War: jingoistic illustration from *The War Illustrated*, Christmas 1917. The caption reads, 'Christmas Box for Fritz. British aeroplanes dropping unwelcome gifts on the German lines in France'.

5.11 'Crackers on the Belgian coast, where British destroyers and monitors contributed surprises to the enemy submarine bases'. Another bellicose caption to an illustration in *The War Illustrated*, Christmas 1917

5.12 The fraternising of troops in Belgium on Christmas Day 1914: a group of German soldiers with two Englishmen, one in a great coat and the other, fourth from the left, wearing a cap-comforter (Imperial War Museum)

offensive spirits of the men; the instructions concluded, 'Friendly intercourse with the enemy, unofficial armistices (e.g. we won't fire if you don't etc) and the exchange of tobacco and other comforts, however tempting and amusing they may be, are absolutely prohibited'.

It is significant that although a few sections of the Second Corps participated in the truce, the majority did not. Elsewhere, however, many officers and men put down their arms and celebrated Christmas and, in some instances, did so side by side with German troops. There was a report that the Germans swapped barrels of beer, which they had taken from a nearby brewery, for British plum puddings. At another part of the front, a Scottish chaplain and a German divinity student held a joint burial service for the dead. In a letter to *The Times* a major from the Leicester regiment recounted how on Christmas Eve, both British and Germans sang carols to each other from their respective trenches and then, on Christmas Day, both officers and men spent an hour talking to the Germans in 'no man's land' and exchanging cigars, cigarettes and papers. Another letter to *The Times*, from a member of the London Rifle Brigade, went into more detail about the events on his sector of the front:

We had rather an interesting time in the trenches on Christmas Eve and Christmas Day. We were in some places less than 100 yards from the Germans and held conversations with them across. It was agreed in our part of the firing line that there would be no firing and no thought of war on Christmas Eve and Christmas Day, so they sang and played to us several of their own tunes and some of ours such as 'Home Sweet Home', 'Tipperary' etc., while we did the same for them. The regiment on our left all got out of their trenches and every time a flare went up they simply stood there, cheered, and waved their hats and not a shot was fired on them. The singing and playing continued all night, and the next day (Christmas) our fellows paid a visit to the German trenches, and they did likewise. Cigarettes, cigars, addresses etc were exchanged and every one, friend and foe, was real good pals. One of the German officers took a photo of English and German soldiers arm-in-arm with exchanged caps and helmets. On Christmas Eve the Germans burned coloured lights and candles along the top of their trenches, and on Christmas Day a football match was played between them and us in front of the trench. They even allowed us to bury all our dead lying in front, and some of them, with hats in their hands, brought in one of our dead officers from behind their trench so that we could bury him decently. They were really magnificent in the whole thing and jolly good sorts. I have now a very different opinion of the Germans. Both sides have started the firing and are already enemies again. Strange it all seems, doesn't it?

The events of Christmas 1914 placed the government and army commanders in a difficult position. Should the fraternisation be publicly condoned or condemned? The German answer was almost immediate. A general order dated 29 December was circulated forbidding fraternisation, and emphasizing that such actions were punishable as high treason. No such order came from the British command at this time, and although Field Marshal Sir John French later wrote that when he was informed about the truce he 'called the local commanders to strict account, which resulted in a good deal of trouble', very few officers appear to have been reprimanded. In any case, it would have been unwise to act too severely because by this time letters from servicemen and even photographs were being published in the British national and local press. Interestingly enough, although the press did not hesitate to record the Christmas truce, they were, by and large, reluctant to express an opinion about it. There were very few editorials on the subject and some publications definitely attempted to ignore the incident. *The War Illustrated*, for example, which gave a highly partisan week-by-week account of the progress of the war, contained no article or comment on the events apart from one small photograph with the caption: 'Phenomenal as it may appear that soldiers fight to the death one day and fraternise the next, it is after all only strictly in accordance with human

5.13 The solitary picture of the 1914 Christmas truce printed in *The War Illustrated*, 16 January 1915

nature. Such incidents are not uncommon in warfare, and occurred in Napoleonic and Russo-Japanese campaigns.'

Despite the apparently lenient attitude on the part of the British High Command towards the Christmas truce, it soon became clear that they were determined there should be no repetition either of the truce or of letters such as that written by the major from the Leicester regiment to *The Times* in which he expressed the view that the Germans 'are jolly, cheery fellows for most of the part and it seems so silly under the circumstances to be fighting them'. Consequently, before Christmas 1915 strict instructions were issued to the troops forbidding any sort of fraternisation. This time the orders were obeyed. Perhaps, in any case, the bitterness of the fighting over the previous twelve months had ensured that neither side would wish to repeat the occasion. In addition, British officers went to great lengths to make certain that their men were too busily engaged in their own Christmas activities to think about peace and goodwill in regard to their opponents. Services were held, carols were sung, and where possible inter-regimental soccer matches were played. Above all, strenuous efforts were made by Quartermasters to provide a traditional Christmas dinner. At times, at the front, this proved extremely difficult. The report of 'A' Battery of the 330th Brigade, fighting near Passchendaele in 1917, mentioned that the Christmas turkeys had not arrived but that rabbits had been used instead and all had gone off very well 'both at guns and wagon line'. Captain Greenwell, writing home to his mother from the Italian front at Christmas 1917, believed that

> The men have had the best Christmas since they left England: it was a huge success. We arranged a football competition – six a side – which kept the Company occupied all the morning and afternoon and caused great excitement and enthusiasm. In order to make the thing go, the officers entered a team, but as we are only six in number we all of us had to play, including myself. It was a bitterly cold day and the Italians must have thought us quite mad. . . .
> Dinners were at 1: the men were all able to sit down and the NCOs waited on them. We gave them port and roast beef with piles of potatoes and greens. The plum puddings were followed by apples, oranges, nuts and cigarettes. Of course beer was out of the question, so we bought some red wine, dosed it up with sugar and lemon, and boiled it into a sort of mulled claret. Later we gave them cold suppers and my Mess cook made them a rum punch, with some vermouth in it and lemon. But the best of all was the arrival of a three or four days' mail in the middle of dinner: it came as a Godsend.

The lesson had been learnt: there were no further unofficial truces either in the First or the Second World Wars, although during the Christmas of 1940 a quite unfounded rumour did circulate through London to the effect that the Germans had not bombed the capital on Christmas Day because some sort of 'gentleman's agreement' had been worked out.

By the time the Second World War started the Christmas truce of 1914 was a vague memory. Very few were aware that it had taken place on such a large scale and, indeed, some believed it was merely a pleasant myth and not an actual event. Both British and American military commanders during the Second World War ensured that all servicemen, wherever they were, were given special treatment at Christmas. The men were kept fully occupied with special film shows and, on some camps, there were special Christmas entertainments with visits from film and variety stars. On occasions, because of hostilities, Christmas

5.14 Soldier with a
Christmas pudding, 17
December 1917 (Imperial
War Museum)

5.15 Neither the pose nor the
Christmas fare alters much:
Gnr H. Hadlow brings in the
Christmas pudding, 20
December 1944 (Imperial
War Museum)

could not be celebrated on the 25th, but usually if this was the case another day
was set aside for the celebrations. For the 2nd Battalion of the East Lancashire
regiment fighting in the jungle of Burma in 1944, Christmas took place on the
28th. There was a dinner delivered by airdrop, of pork, goose, duck, chicken,
plum pudding and four bottles of beer per man. Also the seemingly inevitable
football match took place on the same day. The men serving in 'A' Company of
the First Battalion of the same regiment were fighting in the Ardennes in
Christmas 1944. They were able to celebrate Christmas on the 25th and they too
had a special Christmas dinner, plenty of Belgian beer brought from a nearby
'bistro' and whisky which had been purloined from one of the officers. By the end
of the meal, as the Company report states, 'everyone felt very satisfied and very
soon the men moved slowly back to their various foxholes or farms; but an
obstinate minority kept up a lusty singsong until tea-time'.

For many servicemen, however, as Captain Greenwell had pointed out, the high point of Christmas was the receiving of presents and letters from sweethearts, wives and children back at home. Children were not forgotten, and even if servicemen could not indulge their own sons and daughters at Christmas, they rarely neglected children in the local camp neighbourhood. Special treats and parties were arranged, and Christmas parties at American air and army bases in Britain were particularly popular with children whose sweet and food ration was extremely limited. Even more coveted were the invitations to the parties organised by the allied troops in Western Europe in December 1944. For many of the French, Belgian and Dutch children who had lived under enemy occupation for four Christmases, Christmas was something bewilderingly new. The men went to great lengths, with limited means, to give these children a taste of a traditional Christmas. At one such party arranged by a reconnaisance wing of the Royal Canadian Air Force, 200 Dutch children aged between four and ten were transported to the airbase and given a picture show, a visit from St Nicholas, plenty of presents from a huge Christmas tree and a meal consisting of 1,500 sandwiches, 18 cakes, 500 sausage rolls and – something almost unheard of at that time – ice cream. In addition the children received chocolate bars, sweets and biscuits, all of which had been saved up by the servicemen from the parcels they had received from home. But while this party was taking place, a group of other, less fortunate children gathered and stood outside watching the lucky ones. By the end of the party the number of children outside had grown to about 300 in number. The response of the airmen was to invite the children in, re-lay the tables and start all over again.

Compared with most of the civilians back in Britain, servicemen ate extremely well at Christmas time. A social worker from London wrote in her diary on 19 December, 1943:

> . . . we are pretty well on our beam ends as far as Christmas fare is concerned. Though we all have enough to eat, there is no chance of turkey, chicken or goose, or even the

5.18 Dutch children being lifted into the trucks to go home after the RCAF party

despised rabbit. If we can get a little mutton that is the best we can hope for. There are a few Christmas puddings around but not many. However I managed to get one. This is marvellous because many people have not been able to get any at all. There are shops with three Christmas puddings and 800 registered customers.

The shortages of luxury goods, turkeys, chickens, plum puddings, raisins, fruit, nuts and so on were one of a number of factors which affected the Christmases of families on the home front during the Second World War. The introduction of rationing also limited the range of gifts which could be bought and present buying was mostly of non-coupon goods or those which only had a small coupon value, such as stockings and handkerchieves. There was also a steep rise in the prices of non-rationed Christmas goods, especially toys. But the separation of families by military service, war work or evacuation was of course the major determinant of how Christmas was spent.

Nevertheless, despite the many shortages and the difficulties involved, most families made determined efforts to celebrate the festival. A Mass-Observation survey in December 1941 discovered that only 5% of those questioned believed that Christmas should not be celebrated. The man who argued that there should be no holiday and that 'everybody should work like the Russians' was in a very small minority. Interestingly, all the women taking part in the survey stated that Christmas should be observed, at least to some extent. Most thought it important from 'the children's point of view' and others were even more explicit: 'war or no war this *is* Christmas'. Even those who could not summon up the usual enthusiasm for Christmas still made efforts to save up luxuries and titbits for Christmas Day, and to provide a dinner which had 'some semblance of the habitual Christmas food'. So, a large part of the Christmas preparations in wartime involved waiting in long queues, especially outside food shops, and visiting crowded toy shops in an effort to buy expensive but often shoddy presents for the children.

These efforts to 'make-do' and maintain a traditional Christmas despite the war were portrayed in a short documentary film, *Christmas Under Fire*, made at the end of 1940. The film was first shown in British cinemas in January 1941 but it was also intended for showing in the United States. In fact, as Harry Watt, the producer of the film, later recalled in his autobiography, the film was made at the specific request of the British Ministry of Information who believed that 'what was needed was something to make the American public uncomfortable

5.19 Apart from the black-out, Christmas in Britain in 1939 was not all that different from previous ones, from the point of view of supplies of food and drink: Moussec advertisement, Christmas 1939

5.20 'The Father Christmas of 1939: Same Beard, Same Boots, Same Cloak ... But he Carries a Tin Hat.' *Picture Post*, 23 December 1939 (Pictorial Press)

while they celebrated Christmas'. In other words, it was one of very many attempts made in 1940 and 1941 by the British government to put pressure on the United States to enter the war with Germany.

The film sets out to show the admiring reactions of a supposedly neutral American observer to the way the English cope with Christmas during the blitz of 1940: Quentin Reynolds, an American correspondent for *Collier's Weekly*, was asked to speak the commentary. During the course of the film references are made to the reduced quality of the English family Christmas compared with that enjoyed in the United States, but Reynolds concentrates mainly on the attempts of these families to maintain a traditional Christmas:

It is Christmas Day. I am leaving London tonight and flying to New York. I am taking with me a film despatch. The story of Christmas in England, the year of the blitz, 1940. . . . War or no war, the children of England will not be cheated out of the one day they look forward to all the year. As far as possible this will be an old-fashioned Christmas in England, at least for the children.

It won't be quite the same of course. In England, as in the rest of the civilised world, Christmas has always been the day when the family comes home. Now sons and fathers are fighting in the air, on the sea, and in countries far away. Others will have to

remain at their posts in London or in other cities driving ambulances, fighting fires, patrolling the streets. The war will not stop for Christmas Eve. It will be a Christmas of contrasts; holly and barbed wire, guns and tinsel. . . .
This is not the most cheerful Christmas that ever came to England, but everyone is determined to make it as cheerful as possible. Christmas here this year won't perhaps be the Christmas children in America will be lucky enough to enjoy. England is fighting for her life and even the smallest child understands that.

The film illustrates how, despite bombed theatres, pantomime rehearsals continue in cellars; decorations are mounted in shops whose fronts have been blown out by the blasts of bombs; holly and tinsel adorn barbed wire and gun emplacements; and a Christmas tree brightens up a crowded tube station in which people are sleeping and sheltering. In face of German aggression Britain, in Reynolds's words, 'stands unbeaten, unconquered and unafraid' and does what she 'has done for a thousand years. She worships the Prince of Peace'.

Just as in the nineteenth century, when at Christmas the wealthy were made to remember the sick, the unemployed and the less fortunate living in their neighbourhood, so with *Christmas Under Fire* the British Ministry of Information was setting out to make the Americans feel 'uncomfortable while they celebrated Christmas.' Certainly, the values of Christmas portrayed in this film were those which were readily understood by American audiences. But although some Americans may have felt 'uncomfortable', President Roosevelt in early 1941 was certainly not convinced that he could persuade his country to fight a European war. It was only with the attack on Pearl Harbour later in the year, and Hitler's subsequent declaration of war against the United States in support of his Japanese allies, that American involvement in Europe became certain. The British Prime Minister, Winston Churchill, relieved that America had entered the war and anxious to consult with his new partner, travelled over to

5.21 Decorations are hung in a shop whose windows have been blown out by a bomb. From *Christmas Under Fire* (Imperial War Museum)

5.22 Londoners sheltering in a tube station, Christmas 1940. From *Christmas Under Fire* (Imperial War Museum)

5.23 A child's letter to her father serving in the navy: part of the attempt to make the Americans feel 'uncomfortable while they celebrated Christmas'. From *Christmas Under Fire* (Imperial War Museum)

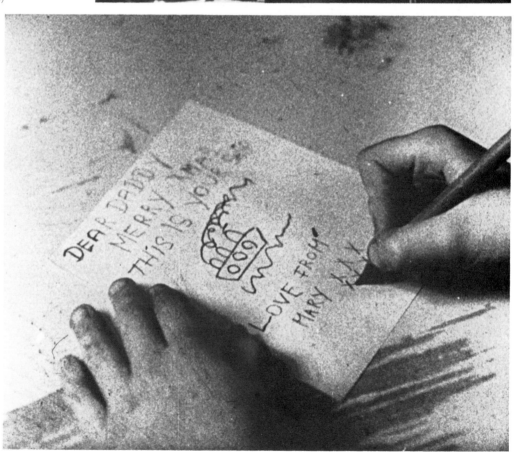

Washington arriving on the 22 December 1941.

Churchill's major public engagement while in the United States was an address to both Houses of Congress on Boxing Day. But during his stay, much publicity was given to the apparent goodwill and fellowship of the two heads of government over the Christmas period. On Christmas Day both men went to church together. As Roosevelt said, 'It is good for Winston to sing hymns with the Methodies'. More significant, perhaps, were the events on Christmas Eve when Roosevelt invited Churchill to attend the lighting of the Christmas tree in the grounds of the White House. Around 30,000 people gathered to celebrate the event, listen to a sermon, sing carols and hear short addresses from both Roosevelt and Churchill. In his few words Churchill urged all Americans to enjoy their Christmas before setting about the formidable task of fighting for victory:

> Let the children have their night of fun and laughter. Let the gifts of Father Christmas delight their play. Let us grown-ups share to the full in their unstinted pleasures before we turn again to the stern task and the formidable years that lie before us, resolved that, by our sacrifice and daring, these same children shall not be robbed of their inheritance or denied their right to live in a free and decent world. And so, in God's mercy, a happy Christmas to you all.

Churchill's appeal for sacrifice was one which appeared to be readily understood by the public both in Britain and the United States. Most people adopted the attitude that in the circumstances they must make the best of a bad job at Christmas. As one woman shopper in Britain remarked when it became

5.24 Roosevelt and Churchill leave the White House for Christmas services at the Foundry Methodist Church, 25 December 1941. With the two leaders are: extreme left, Lord Beaverbrook, British Minister of Supply; Mrs Roosevelt; and, on the extreme right, Gen. Edwin M. Watson, aide to the President. (Bettmann Archive/BBC Hulton Picture Library)

Two Egg Sauces for Christmas

A rich and flavoursome sauce can turn a plain dish into a party one, and give a festive touch to a homely meal. Let tasty egg sauces add extra niceness and nourishment to your Christmas fare. Serve lemon sauce with the Christmas pudding, and a refreshingly sharp sauce with the meat, fish or poultry. Dried eggs are easy to *get*, easy to *cook*, and easy on the *purse* as well.

LEMON SAUCE

Ingredients: 2 level tablespoons dried egg, 2 level tablespoons flour, 1 pint milk, 1½ oz. sugar, 6 drops lemon essence, *or* 6 drops rum essence, *or* 1-2 level teaspoons grated nutmeg. *Method:* Mix the flour and egg together and blend to a smooth cream with a little of the milk. Boil the remainder and pour on to the blended mixture. Return to the pan and boil for 5 minutes. Add the sugar, flavouring and serve.

SHARP SAUCE

Ingredients: 1 level tablespoon dried egg, dry, 2 level tablespoons flour, 1 level teaspoon each of mustard, sugar and salt, pepper, ½ pint milk or vegetable water, 1 oz. margarine, 4 tablespoons vinegar. *Method:* Mix the flour, egg, mustard, sugar, salt and pepper. Mix to a smooth paste with a little of the milk or vegetable water. Boil remaining liquid, pour on to the blended flour, return to pan and bring to the boil. Boil for 5 minutes. Remove from heat and add margarine. Mix well and add vinegar.

'EGGS IS EGGS'!

DE 14

clear that she would have no chicken for Christmas 1942, 'We'll just have to put up with it. The war s more important than Christmas'.

Of course, all government departments throughout the year made efforts to urge the civilian population to save and economise, and at Christmas time these efforts were redoubled. The Ministry of Food devised recipes aimed at enabling people to have traditional Christmas fare made from untraditional ingredients. Suggestions for making Christmas cakes without fresh butter and eggs abounded and one recipe even urged the use of grated potato instead of dried fruit. In 1944 a Christmas recipe from the Ministry of Food involved using dried egg custard for making crème brulée. In December 1942 a Potato Fair was organised on the bombed site of a London store in Oxford Street. Customers signed a pledge promising 'as my Christmas gift to sailors who have to bring our bread that I will do all I can to eat home-grown potatoes'.

In the United States there were similar appeals to civilians to help in the war effort. At Christmas 1942 MGM studios issued a publicity photograph of their

5.25 Ministry of Food recipes, December 1944

5.26 MGM publicity Christmas 1942: 'It's a wartime Christmas for 5 year old Margaret O'Brien MGM starlet. On a small unlighted tree Margaret receives Savings Bonds and Stamps in lieu of dolls and toys.' (National Film Archive London)

five year old star, Margaret O'Brien, enjoying her austerity Christmas. Instead of dolls and toys on her unlit Christmas tree were Saving Bonds and Stamps. This picture of O'Brien was given extensive coverage not only in the United States but also in Britain, where her film, *Journey for Margaret*, in which she played a girl orphaned in the London blitz, had been a box office success. In the film, the girl is found by an American correspondent who subsequently takes her back with him to the safety of America.

The major grievance in Britain at Christmas time was not so much the shortages but the 'black-out', a factor which affected shoppers the whole year round. The dangers of tripping over kerbstones and trying to find one's way in the dark were greater irritants, so Mass-Observation surveys concluded, than anything else. In the early days of the war especially, when the 'black-out' was unfamiliar and shoppers inexperienced, there was often much confusion. One woman recalled how on a Saturday afternoon before the Christmas of 1939, she decided to visit her local Marks and Spencer's store in Romford, Essex:

> The shop has a wide front, with three entrances, but only one entrance was in use, on account of the black-out. There was complete pandemonium at the door. The wet crowds from the street were surging inwards, and the hot crowds from the store were surging outwards, and the perspiring little manager stood in the middle, swearing and waving his arms inadequately. It took quite ten minutes to get through the door. Even when I was in, it was almost impossible to see my friend or to buy anything. Practically the entire shop was blocked with people waiting to get out. When I joined the queue at about 4.30 people were getting very bad-tempered. At last the manager decided to open all the doors. In order to do that, and at the same time conform with black-out regulations, the lights at the front of the shop had to be switched off. This immediately caused panic . . . 'It's a raid . . . They're here' etc etc. There was a sudden rush for the doors, and I had no desire but to flow out with the rest.
> What a relief to get out into the rain!

Of course, there were complaints about shortages, the high price of toys, profiteering and the 'black market'. Shoppers in their eagerness to obtain the best for their families often resorted to bribing shop assistants. One employee in a large London food store estimated that one customer in twelve offered 'something' for Christmas and in another West End store in 1944 notices were hung asking shoppers not to offer gratuities, which would not only put the shop assistants in an embarrassing position but would also make them liable to dismissal. Very often complaints were not directed towards the government, or shop managers or, for that matter, 'black marketeers' but rather against neighbours who seemed better off. Even Vera Hodgson, a London social worker, evinced some bitterness when she wrote in her diary at Christmas 1943, 'the shops are full of expensive goods which only munition workers can afford'. One of the reasons why American GIs were resented by some was that they appeared to have plenty of money to spend on Christmas goods and were never short of Christmas turkeys, whereas poultry of any sort was extremely scarce for the British population in the later years of the war.

Sharper still were the reactions of those who discovered that some people lower down the social scale were having a more extravagant time than themselves at Christmas. The report of a Mass-Observation interviewer at Christmas 1941 included the complaints of one middle class woman:

5.27 GI with children at Harrods Toy Fair, Christmas 1945: notice the empty shelves on the extreme left. (Harrods)

> I was calling on the D's on Xmas afternoon about the raffle – he's my dustman you know – and do you know they were having a pair of chickens for their dinner! I asked her afterwards how they could afford it, and she said 'Oh, we do without a bit each week, then we have enough for Christmas time'. Just think of it, and he's got a weak stomach, and those miserable pale children – I would be ashamed to have a child like those – and yet she makes them go without proper food for weeks just so as to make a show at Christmas! I think it's wicked. I don't know what you can *do* in the face of stupidity like that.

In the final analysis, however, just as in peacetime, the manner in which Christmas Day was spent usually depended on where you lived and the means at your disposal. Whereas many townspeople in the later years of the war were making do with stewing beef or mutton for Christmas dinner, those who had some sort of garden and were able to keep chickens managed a more traditional Christmas dinner. Again, although many families could not afford luxuries or did without them others, like the member of a well-to-do middle class family, could bemoan the fact that they had been unable to obtain any brandy for the celebrations on Christmas Day in 1941. This lady's account of Christmas is in marked contrast to that of the poor beleaguered British portrayed by Quentin Reynolds in *Christmas Under Fire*.

> At half past 12 we were all sent up to get dressed and come down in time for the Xmas dinner. Punctually at one o'clock, the gong was rung, and we proceeded into the dining room to have our dinner, which was much like a peacetime Xmas dinner. We had a turkey with bread sauce, gravy, roast potatoes, carrots and cabbage. And afterwards, the traditional Christmas pudding with brandy sauce. But for the first time I can remember no brandy was poured over the Xmas pudding, and it was not lit before being cut into slices. This was due to the cook being unable to get any brandy this year. We also had a bottle of graves with our dinner, and two glasses were sent into the kitchen for the maids.

5.28 Sentimental home-coming. *Graphic*, Christmas 1880

5.29 'Home Again! The Hero's Return at Christmastide'. *The War Illustrated*, 25 December 1915

Whatever their situation, whether at home in Britain and the United States, fighting in Europe, Africa, Burma or the Philippines, or, since the end of the Second World War, in Korea, Vietnam or the Falkland Islands, people have always made strenuous efforts to observe Christmas. In wartime, even more than in times of peace, consideration is given to those away from home, and the desire to be with one's family is even greater. Illustrations of soldiers and sailors returning home at Christmas appeared over and over again in one form or another in the nineteenth century and during the First World War. As a writer in *The Times* on 24 December 1917 remarked, 'Leave is an event at any time, a longed and hoped-for, dreamed-of event, but at no time so much as when the precious 14 days include Christmas Day'.

Like the longing for one's family, the desire for peace seems to intensify at Christmas. Private William Tapp, who took part in the Christmas truce of 1914, put his finger on the paradox of Christmas in wartime when he wrote of the Germans in his diary, 'They say they are not going to fire again if we don't but of course we must and shall do, but it doesn't seem right to be killing each other at Xmas time'. This feeling that 'it doesn't seem right' to be at war at Christmas is

AFTER THE TURMOIL OF WAR: THE TENDERNESS OF DOMESTIC PEACE.

deeply embedded in the Western consciousness. Perhaps it was no accident that the cry, right at the start of the First World War, was that the war would be over by Christmas. Again, during the Second World War, the Allied Commander-in-Chief, General Eisenhower, had a bet with the British Army Commander, General Montgomery, that Christmas 1944 would see the ending of hostilities in Europe.

Both Eisenhower and the optimists of 1914 were to be disappointed, but considering the importance of Christmas in the yearly cycle and the values attached to it, perhaps one can understand the reasoning behind these predictions. Despite all manner of hardships, Christmas, for practising and non-practising Christians alike, is a festival which is not only observed by special dinners and presents but also contains within it deeply held values. One man living in London at the height of the blitz in 1940, when asked whether he would be observing Christmas, replied that he most certainly would because

> it's probably the thing that's most precious to the British people than all their so-called ideals and democracy and all the rest of it. I mean that seriously. I suppose it's because the British Christmas is the embodiment of all the ideals we are fighting for.

Many Americans would have said the same about the American Christmas and the American war effort. Christmas becomes in wartime a symbol of our better selves and all that is best in our civilization.

Postscript

Well, how did you enjoy your Christmas? As you take down the tree, put the decorations away for another year, glance guiltily at the empty bottles in the yard and consider your cheque book with growing remorse, does it all seem to have been worth while?

There are some doubts: the children didn't live up to that little dream we had of them as excited angels on Christmas morning; they weren't as pleased with those expensive presents as they should have been and Peter ate all those sweets and was unable to enjoy his Christmas dinner; it was great that we managed to persuade Uncle Bob to come but one had forgotten he was quite so talkative and so boring; and it was a pity that we had a row after the Brown's party on Boxing Day – I was only *talking* to that blonde who seemed so interested in the computer business!

The trouble with Christmas is that we expect so much from it. There is always the gap between expectation and the event itself, between ideal and reality. It's easy to be cynical about Christmas, to emphasize the bells of the cash registers instead of the churches and to point to the paradox of the celebration of the transcendental with plum puddings and brandy. Few of us would wish with Charles Dickens 'that Christmas lasted the whole year through'.

Yet, within a few months, we shall be anticipating and preparing for next Christmas. We will remember only the best things about the Christmas just past: the beauty of the midnight service, the excitement of Christmas morning and the heightened sense of fellowship and family unity. Perhaps next year Christmas really will be like it used to be!

BIBLIOGRAPHICAL NOTE

In the course of writing this book we have read very many 'Christmas' books. We must make mention here of M. Harrison, *The Story of Christmas* (1951) which contains a detailed account of pre-Christian Christmases; J.A.R. Pimlott, *The Englishman's Christmas* (1978) which looks at Christmas from the earliest times to the present-day; James H. Barnett, *The American Christmas* (1954), a sociological study which although by now somewhat dated, contains much interesting material; M. Brown and S. Seaton, *Christmas Truce* (1984), an excellent account of the events on the Western Front at Christmas 1914. We should also like to acknowledge the oral accounts of past Christmases in P. Thompson, *The Edwardians* (1975) and E. Roberts, *A Woman's Place* (1984).

INDEX